MC – Squared:
Motivational Conversations
with Marvette Camille

Order this book online at www.trafford.com
or email orders@trafford.com

Most Trafford titles are also available at major online book retailers.

Printed in the United States of America.

ISBN: 978-1-4269-8996-4 (sc)
ISBN: 978-1-4269-8997-1 (e)

Trafford rev. 09/21/2011

 www.trafford.com

North America & international
toll-free: 1 888 232 4444 (USA & Canada)
phone: 250 383 6864 ◆ fax: 812 355 4082

Acknowledgements

Thanks seem such an inadequate way to express one's true feelings of gratitude when the encouragement and support of others leads to the realization of a dream. However, since it is the word that is presently available, I spread it generously around to all those who helped in giving birth to my first book. Thanks go firstly to my creator who saw it fit to loan me this wonderful outlet for the expression of my most profound thoughts and feelings. A big thank you also goes out to those who have encouraged me to make what I write available to others in this way. It would be remiss of me not to mention some special people by name; the sister of my heart and childhood friend Dawn (Audrey-Dawn) Minott, Karaine Smith-Holness, the girl I call my twin since we are alike in so many ways, and someone I have never met in person, Sharilyn Pringle, who I met through my writings on Facebook; who have long championed the cause for me to publish.

Thanks as well to my friend Gary Hyde who has been my quiet voice of reason and calm to combat my sometimes frenzied demeanor throughout the process. Extra special thanks to my beautiful sister Marlo (Annie) Facey-Young for helping me to edit; being my second pair or eyes was such a great help. A very special thank you to my childhood - super talented friend, Andrea (June) Lee, whose handiwork graces the cover of my book, accompanied by the beautiful picture taken by Karaine. There are so many others that are not mentioned by name but have played a huge role in encouraging me to undertake this project, but you know yourselves so please accept my heartfelt thanks. ***Much thanks all.***

Contents

Chapter 6 : Learning From Life's Imperfections 95

Chapter 7 : Strength and Triumph — 115

Chapter 1

Thankfulness and Well-Being

"As you inhale fresh air into willing lungs, think about the awesomeness of the universe and the gift of life. Be thankful for yet another day, as you work towards optimizing on the gifts bestowed on you; loving yourself and others a little more, frowning a lot less, and seeing life's challenges as merely a way of showing you just how precious life is. You have the power to make each day what YOU want it to be" (MC).

Rejuvenation

Buoyed by life's **simplest** of things,
my soul's so **peaceful** i'm levitating –
lifted to a space where walls are invisible,
walking on water is possible,
imaginations have no ceilings
and stress evaporates like butter against a too-persistent sun.

Taken to the highest of pinnacles –
experiencing visions of a **calm** that seeps through **relaxed** pores
and leak into organs lay prostrate –
ready to be shaken and stirred into juices of serenity;
deep breaths of the cleanest air, and an atmosphere of **tranquility.**

A mind transported from things mundane to inhabit a place of **mind-massaging**
contentment.
That forces from me, a litany of mind –
Songs that set my heart free to skip like a happy child,
and to roam **free** in terrains of smoothness and bliss.

Rejuvenated, refreshed, renewed; ready to conquer my fears,
fulfill my dreams, be a blessing to others,
and to **evolve** into the very best of me….

NAMING your BLESSINGS one by one

We get up every morning; sometimes forgetting to thank our creator for allowing our eyes to open to behold yet another day,

We complain before we say thanks, we bellyache about the jobs we have that others would do anything to get. We place so much emphasis on the negatives in our lives that they overshadow the many blessings that should be highlighted.

We moan and groan over the things that are not going right in our lives, forgetting to remember that the one who created us sometimes allow us to come upon obstacles thereby diverting us from a path that's leading us to self-destruction. We do everything except give thanks for life and health and strength.

If we stop for just a minute of the day and step outside ourselves to see how truly blessed we are, instead of merely existing to add to what we already have - all the time forgetting to be grateful that we have been able to achieve so much, then we would be able to SEE our blessings for what they are, and spend less time complaining and more time being thankful and appreciative of those things we *do* have!!.

You didn't have to wake up this morning, but you *did*, you didn't have to have a job to go to, but you *do*. You could be lying in a hospital bed somewhere, but you are *not*. Take a step back from your rushed existence and look around you on all of your blessings; No I mean *really* stop and look ……..they *are* many; aren't they just????.

C *R *E *A *T* I *V *I* T* Y

Rising like a phoenix from beneath the need of compelling expression. Ready to burst forth, to escape a mind overflowing with intense *creativity.*

Words dripping from swelled pen tips, art derived from aroused easels ready to burst into an orgasmic array of sexy colours.

A trickle of heart-leaks that flow from nothingness into spring-wells of beauty and light - illuminated by droplets of what has been purged from your innermost.

Painting deep resonances that are stained by the compulsion to capture the beauty that lies in everything. Nude eyes ready to be clothed in visions of saturated imaginings – giving birth to brightly-dressed productions of the mind.

Soul-drenched spark lets, soaked in all that's in the depth of you – waiting to be delivered of things buried deeper than you even knew. The spirit-cuddled escape of your most profound you – bleeding from unclogged brain cells, opened heart, and a free spirit, as you make expressions of self, like *only* you can….

Forever came TODAY....

Been searching for "it" for oh so long
that elusive thing Iv'e **always** wanted
but has been **nowhere** in sight....

It sometimes feel so **far** away
but sometimes it's **just** outside my grasp
I'm **tasting** it, i'm **touching** it
but for now it lives **only** in my **imaginings**
just waiting to be explored....

It's postponed, delayed, put off, placed on hold;
While I twiddle my thumbs, put off the inevitable
And wait a while even though I'd like my future to start right now.

I am living my now, but I want my future today, when I can live my dreams instead of
just dreaming them
and be happy **now**, instead of waiting for tomorrow.
I am living in my now, but I want the fruits of my forever....**today**.

That Space in Time

There comes a time when the place in which you find yourself is either *the* place you want to be, the place you *wish* you were or the place you **never** want to be again.

When your life takes you to that place you never want to be again, make sure you internalize the lessons you *will* inevitably learn, *hard* though they may be.

When it takes you to that place you *wish* you were, do whatever it takes in your power to get there, as in my way of thinking, wishes are just the flip side of whatever reality *we* make of them.

When you are all warm and cozy in that *place* you *want* to be, cherish those days, embrace them, and keep them for future reference when you get back to that place in your life where you never want to be again.

All our experiences are simply the space we are in at a certain time. If we learn from the times we wish we could completely wipe from our memory banks, and *cherish* those times we wish would stay, then as our lives rotate on its cyclical axis and we go back to those inevitable not so fun spaces and places in time, we will *learn from* and *appreciate* our lives and experiences all the more.

In whatever space in time you find yourself, do with it what will result in the optimum experience by taking whatever it is you *can* learn, and filing it away for future use. As you live, and grow, and strive and BE, chalk up *all* those places and spaces you have found yourself in - as the building blocks to the course of your life as your journey continues……..

God's Opened Doors (GOD)

We push our way through doors that are barricaded for a reason
and mow down those that should be left alone
We run blindly through ones that are slightly ajar; barreling our way through,
and skip merrily through wide opened ones that lead us to NOWHERE

The wide opened doors welcoming though they may be, are oftentimes not the ones that are opened for us, and the ones that are slightly opened are oftentimes not pushed fully open, as all that's inside is not ready to be explored by us.

God opens those doors He deems necessary for us to enter into; the doors we think are not wide enough, or are not painted in bright, pretty colours are the ones that lead us into God's PERFECT will for our lives. There may not be whistles and bells at the entrance of God's opened doors to beckon us in, but if those ARE the ones you SHOULD walk through, then the still, small voice WILL guide you to it.

The doors God open for us are paved with the right tiles of perseverance, a sufficient path of guidance, a GREAT walkway of long-suffering, and a PERFECT map of directions, that NO one can close!!!!.

In God's plans for us, the doors that remain closed SHOULD be left as they are, no matter how BADLY we want them opened. Don't push through, mow down, run blindly, or skip merrily through doors even if they are wide opened, as the ones prepared JUST for you are the ONLY ones that will bring you *true*, lasting *joy* and *peace* – the kind that ONLY God can grant you.

Finding Contentment Where you Find Yourself

We tend to wait for future plans to come to fruition for us to find contentment in our lives. In the interim, we forget to *live* in the moment. Whilst ambition, goals and resolutions are great with respect to where we want to be in either the near or distant future, it is *imperative* to find contentment in where you are at a particular moment in time.

Complacency and the "acceptance of one's fate" are mere cop outs in my estimation. They are simply excuses not to go after one's dreams and aspirations. On the other hand however, if you are not sitting on your hands, or wringing them and saying "woe is me" as you wait on the world to pay you what you think you're owed, then it means you are where you are now, but working to get to where you want to be in the future.

While you are at *this* point, find contentment in your "here and now" and do not wait until your "later" or "your what is to come" as today is the *only* day you are promised, and for you, tomorrow may never come. Do not wait to be content when you get to your ideal size or weight, your highest academic achievement, your dream house, car, or spouse. Live for today and be contented in the fact that you have life, love and good health.

If tomorrow never comes for you, let it be said that you lived and died happy where you *were*, while you worked towards achieving your other goals. After all, the contentment you are feeling today, can only help to propel you into the ultimate contentment that you will feel after the realization of those goals and dreams right?

Contentment with where you are *now* is crucial as even when you get to where you *want* to be, there is always someplace else you will desire to get to, as life is a cycle, and not even self-actualization makes one stop hoping and dreaming, planning and setting goals. Find contentment in the you - you are *today*, as you work towards becoming the you, you wish to become *tomorrow*.

Introspection... Something to Consider

Life will always be here whether or not we are. There is always something happening and stuff will always be swirling around, as this is a part of the definition of *L I F E*. The hustle and bustle around us is here to stay, having to keep up with the "grind" will forever be a part of our existence, whether or not we are working for others or plowing our way through and working for ourselves.

There will always be the need to improve our lives, be it financially, academically, socially and even spiritually. Amidst the hustle and bustle of the world we are in, the noise that constantly surrounds us, the confusion, the misery, the upheaval, the disappointments, the feelings of cognitive dissonance when things you expect to be one way turns out to be something else; when your plans get side-tracked and when everything seem to be in chaos, maybe it's just time to stop and be with *you*.

Turning one's thoughts inwards and trying to get to know yourself better, spending time reflecting on what you want, and more so what you *need*, can be nothing but a good thing. Sometimes what seems to be the biggest, most difficult, unsolvable issue in the universe that is boggling your mind would be so much simpler if you just stopped in the midst of life's ups and downs just to smell the proverbial roses.

Spend some time "doing" you. It may seem that in the mad rush that is your life, that you just *cannot* find the time to stop and share yourself with you. However, taking the time to stop and think, serves as a form of rejuvenation for *both* the mind and the soul, even if after just a little time with you, your body is still not completely rested.

It affords you the opportunity to re-think your priorities making your mind even a little bit clearer and allowing you to place things in their correct perspective. It removes or at the very least, lessens the pressure of the seemingly insurmountable "stuff" that you have to be dealing with; or take you to a space in yourself where you can be accepting even if things are not going the way you want them to go at the present moment.

Take an hour, a day, a weekend, a week, whatever time you can realistically afford to take and do some introspection. It doesn't have to mean that you always have to physically remove yourself from the daily "grind" as I can imagine some of your minds are now going around in circles thinking I cant even find the time to scratch my head, where am I going to find the time to take a day, a weekend or a week just to spend time with me?"

But thankfully, like prayer, introspection can be done almost anywhere at any time, it's just that you may achieve more optimal results if you take your physical self away from the hustle and bustle of life and be one with you and your mind. As it has been said so many times, the mind is a ***powerful thing***. As such, getting your head space where it ought to be whether you are in a crowd or by yourself, is for me, an imperative part of making my life better, as I tend to the business of living.

Try some introspection sometime today, this week, this month, THIS YEAR, and see if it doesnt help you to have a better, healthier, clearer outlook on the things that have been stressing you, that seem impossible, unreachable and unattainable, or something or someone you thought you could NOT live with or without up until now.

Happy introspecting; go get into your own head, heart and soul and I can almost guarantee you WILL find out something about you that you either forgot, or didn't even know about yourself in the first place and that can **only** serve to improve the quality of your life.

Have You Met You?

Have you met you; spent time with you?
Did you discover what makes you happy?

Are you spending time with you, getting to know you?
Do you pamper you, praise you, and recognize your own awesomeness?

Are you relishing your achievements and enjoying the fruits of your labour?
Do you acknowledge your own worth and admit your greatness?

If not, you need to stop and meet you! Take time out to spend with you as you get to
know, discover, pamper, recognize, laugh, be contented, relish and enjoy you….you *are*

worth it!!.

There Comes A Time....

When you HAVE to grow up

When you have to remove those things and people from your life that are dead weight and unnecessary baggage

When the excuses of yesterday are no longer acceptable

When you HAVE to pay closer attention to the lessons life is teaching you

When you have to take RESPONSIBILITY for your own mess and stop passing it on to the things and people around you

When you have to let go of those things you thought you *needed* but realize are just obstacles to your growth

When you have to recognize your **worth**, and demand that you be treated *accordingly.*

When you take back that which was taken from you

When you release your stronghold on life's foolishness and *move on*

When you step up to the plate and *own* your mistakes

When you need someone

When you arc that someone somebody needs

When you *let go* and let God

When you allow yourself to stop being so tough and just let someone take care of you

When you accept your humanness and therefore that you are fallible

When you listen to others and accept that you *do not* know it all

When you learn to let go of your idea of complete control, knowing that you will *never* be able to control *everything!.*

There comes a time:

To just be you

"do" you

be with you

accept you

When you allow yourself to cry, and need without feeling as if you made yourself vulnerable

When you mean what you say and say what you mean

When you take a deep breath and exhale, releasing all the bad karma that's in your existence.

There comes a time when……..it's just time……

The Still, Small Voice (TSSV)

You **hear** it ever so **clearly**; although the octave is so small you may miss it if you are not too careful. There is a HUGE possibility that it will get drowned out by all the noise that surrounds you in the day to day grind of life.

But it pushes through all the **garbage**, telling you what you **should and should not** do, and being the voice that propels you, the conscience that guides you, the balm that calms you, the **extra** "pick me up" that you need to get up and go.

However, we use this voice conveniently, only listening to it when it is saying what we want to hear. When it goes against what we want to do, even when we **know** it's not the right thing for us, we deliberately drown it out with our doubts and fears, and stubbornness.

Then when we get bitten in the butt, we ask the million dollar question "Lord, where were you?" when he was right there in your ear as usual, directing you as to which way to go and what to do.

This world is **so** full of **noise** that invades both our conscious as well as our sub-conscious, that it necessitates the stopping and listening to TSSV that allows us to rely on the direction of one who **sees** and **knows** all things before they happen, and so who therefore can help us to PREVENT avoidable heartaches and unnecessary pain.

Unlike all the noise around us, TSSV is not insistent and overbearing, but it's constant and steady, and if we but **listen**, even from time to time, we'll find that there's not so much need for "if I had knowns" and "why oh why did I do thats" in our lives. It doesn't infiltrate and take over our lives, since it allows us to use the ability to choose that we are given by the creator, but it is ALWAYS there like that trusted friend that you can **always** count on when you **need** them.

STOP....and **listen** for a change, to that **still small voice**!. The difference it will make in your life will be **more than worth it!**

What will "IT" Take?

Will it be the changing of one car for a newer model
the improvement on the man in your life as you "upgrade"
the moving from that "starter house" to your "dream house"
the PhD, the biggest, most expensive and flashy pieces of jewelry that money can buy?

Will it be the baby, the wife, the promotion, or will it be the ability to travel **anywhere** in the world you want to on a whim with nothing like expenses or commitments to hinder you? Will it take an earthquake, a hurricane, a blizzard, a plane crash, a "rude awakening", a close-call, a near-death experience for you to reach deep down inside you and find the peace of mind, heart and soul that you have been **long** searching for?

The thing with waiting on the aforementioned to take place is that while you **wait**, time is passing you by; time you will **never** again see, or be able to get back to do what you could have and **should** have done **yesterday** had you forgotten about the "ifs, "buts" and maybes" and seized the day, **literally**!.

Will you see tomorrow, can you safely bet on it? what about next week, month, year? will you be here? Think about this when next you try to placate yourself with platitudes of what amounts to plain ole' bull; if you spend all your today's "iffing" and butting, what will you get done? will your dreams be realized? will your aspirations be reached?

If you find yourself blessed enough to open your eyes to another brand, spanking new day, you OWE it to yourself to stop waiting on the "next big thing" to happen in your life to propel you into a mode of doing what needs to get done so you can achieve what to me is the **most important** thing in this life; a space where outside of **all** you can and **will** achieve; outside of being self-actualized, you can find the peace inside that can sustain you if you **ever** have to live without all those "things" you think you need to have to make you HAPPY!!!!.

What will it take for you to get to **that** place? ask yourself that all-important question **today**, and go **find** it, **whatever** that "it" may be.

Eliminate the Dead Weight

Hhmm, I'm thinking that there are **many** people that we hang onto for **dear** life who are MERELY dead weight in our lives. They serve **no** purpose other than to fuel our negativity, and to create drama and strife, **all** day **every** day, almost without fail.

They come in **many** forms; as our parents, spouses, siblings and friends. Unfortunately for us, we have convinced ourselves or have been convinced by conventions that **simply** because someone gave birth to us, or donated their sperm to our DNA that we **have** to have them in our close inner circle no matter how **toxic**, and spirit-killing they may be.

You stay in **dead**, **bad**, **done** relationships because of the children, because you are afraid to be alone, because the validation of yourself **has** to come through being with someone else, or because you don't want to "waste" the many years you have spent with that person by getting up and **leaving**, no matter how **horribly** that person treats you and how **low** s/he makes you feel about **you**, about **life**, and about the **future**. The children have and **will** see the disrespect, the hate and resentment and it **only** serves to make them form **unhealthy** relationships themselves. The years you **claim** to be "wasting" will just turn into even **more** wasted years, and you will find you will **have** to leave in the long run, after having spent **many more** years anyway, if you get to leave that is, as you may end up dead.

Some of us have siblings who are **worse** than **enemies**! Whose **only** purpose in life is to make our existence a **living hell**. There is **nothing** we like about them, **nothing** we can think of that is **good** about them, and **all** they **ever** bring to our lives is **misery** and **constant heartache**!.

Then there are those so-called "friends" who when you're around them all you **ever** feel is **negative** energy that **pervades** your **entire** being. All they **ever** do is belly-ache, gossip, and **woe is me**; **never** with a positive word of encouragement to make your day or your existence better. They **suck** the very **air** out of **any** room they enter, and **destroy** an ambiance merely by entering it.

None of us can choose our family, and although we all hold hands and "kumbayah" about "blood being thicker than water," if the blood is so **thick** so that it clogs your arteries and leave you **half-dead**, then **who needs** it? Who **needs** "friends" you **have** to sigh and gear-up yourself to be in their presence, and having to sigh *again*, and "de-dramatize" and "de-funkify" your existence *every time* you exit their presence?

The *only* person you *have* to *always* be around is *you*, everyone else should be brought into your inner circle because they are a complement to your existence, and if they help you in your **growth**, help to pick you up, instead of *always* managing to make you feel down no matter the mood you were in before you experienced their toxic presence.

I am *sure* you *do not* have to look too far to identify the *dead weight* in **your** circle. Do *more* than merely identify them though; love them if you *must*, but keep them at arm's length and minimize your contact with them. If there is someone in your life that the *mere* thought of them changes your mood for the worse, gives you *bad* heart-palpitations at even the *mention* of their name, makes you want to *run and hide*, then it means you need to *ditch* the dead weight!

It may sound really harsh, but who needs someone (whomever they may be) whose *only* purpose in your life is to *poison* and *ruin* all your *moments* no matter how hard you try to have peace around you?   I've learnt that not *all* the people we *love*, we *have* to like, and that not *everyone* you're related to, you *have* to relate to - so do yourselves a *big* favour, and rid yourself of the dead weights around you and see if life won't be *that much more lighter for it!*.

ELEMINATE THE DEAD WEIGHT FOLKS.

Stopping to Smell Life's Roses

Slow down will you? What sense does it make if you work so hard to achieve all you have, yet have no time to enjoy it? While you are so busy on the hunt searching for material things, do not forget to enjoy those things in life that really matter.

Ambition is a good thing, so is the need to succeed, but all that means nothing if you have no one to share it with, or if you cannot find the time to share it with the very people you are working so hard to provide for.

Find the equilibrium; strike that balance in your life where you can get to the place where you not just succeed, but where you can actually sit back and positively benefit from that success.

Life goes by so quickly. In almost no time flat the kids grow up, the years turn into decades, and there does not exist a rewind or replay button for life. So will you do it? Will you stop to smell the roses, inhale life's pleasures, savour the sunset and welcome the sunrise? You *really* should....

Cruise Control

The rev is off as I ease my foot off the accelerator

as i'm in cruise control

The gas is less, the brake is more as I slow it *way* down

cause i'm in cruise control

I'm not trying to pass the guy on right and beat the girl on the left

as i'm in cruise control

I'm relaxed in the driver's seat with no road rage

cause i'm in cruise control

There's no pedal to the metal and no horns blaring

as i'm in cruise control

There's no hair standing on end, no excess blood rushing to my brain

when i'm in cruise control

The brakes are on, the engine is cool

when i'm in cruise control.

By all means, occasionally drive on the fast path of your life's journey, but make *sure* there are those days when you are *just cruising* - as you take the *necessary* time out to venture into the *calmer*, *sweeter*, *kinder* side of life....

Chapter 2

PURPOSE, HARMONY AND RENEWAL

"Believe wholeheartedly that your destiny is a perfect combination of the purpose for which you were created and the way in which you execute your own existence. Spend more time living your destiny and less time worrying about it; expending your energy in renewing your love and zeal for life" (MC).

PURPOSE....

I have been through paths travelled by others, done what has already been done, seen what has been placed in front of me to see and I have wondered; wondered just what *my* purpose is supposed to be.

But as I open my eyes to *yet* another day I am so fortunate to see, the struggle is not as bad as it was yesterday. It's sitting squarely on my shoulder, pointing its bony fingers in my face, screaming in my ear and trampling all over my feet, but I am now up to the challenge – ready to meet it head on.

Why am I here? It's plain to see, not to merely exist simply because I am already here, not to cop to the ideas of others, not when I am smart enough to create a path of my own making.

My purpose for being placed in a complex world filled with mystery, love, hate and innovation, pointing me to a journey to becoming *me*; not what the world wants me to be, not what others expect of me, not what conventions dictate, but to be what I was *created* to be.

I hope you find your purpose, as only then will you be able to complete your journey to you….

"Checking Out"

I sit and stare at the hollow space that exists inside my head, that space that now pervades the place from which my mind has temporarily taken flight. I twist and turn from that iffy place of not knowing just exactly where to go or what to do next, and my mind sits back on its hind legs as it hibernates in its effort to re-vamp and rejuvenate.

The shifting earth beneath me offers no real port of rest for my wayward thoughts as they wander around outside of me in search of peace and a semblance of tranquility that I seek in order to calm my rapidly changing moods, and my forever-moving brain cells that keep me un-naturally busy as I try not to think faster than I can breathe.

As I take myself away from me to catch a quick breather, I remind myself that this is merely a respite from my present reality, as I seek what is necessary to propel me to my next adventure and that "something" which I seek, as I set out on the other leg of my journey.

I'm checking out, i'm applying some "brain freeze," – but only for a lil while, as staying too long in "chill-ville" will affect all those important things I still have left to do. I'm "checking out" of the revolving door of life's outs and ins, but will press the "in button" just as soon as I get done chasing my restless mind trying to find that which I so desperately seek....i'm checking out but ONLY for a few, as soon I will get back to the business of living….

Be PRESENT For your OWN Reality

Eyes opened, mind alert, heart receptive, brain cells ready to think *only* on the *positive*. It is just about that time when you need to simply let go, own and live your life, and for that, there is no time like the present.

Never be an absentee member in your own existence, but be present for your ride through life, as being absent from your own existence is way too sad to even contemplate. Instead, consciously live your *best* life every day you are blessed to see.

Stop being swept up with whatever tide that happens to float by as you wrap yourself in the cloak of "whatever happens-happens" and "so be it." "Whatever will be" does not have to be, if you play an active role in directing your own life.

Some believe that our destinies have already been pre-determined but I believe that you can most certainly chart your path to your *own* destiny by channeling your thoughts in the direction you want your life to follow.

Never give others the power and ability to dictate the route your life will take; take the cues from your own heart, dreams and goals for yourself. It is from that platform of conscious presence in your own future that you will get to the place where you are the driver of your own life instead of a spectator who is merely along for the ride to nowhere in particular. Take a hold of life and create the reality you not just want, but that you *deserve*!!.

I DONT really know you....Yet I DO

I don't really know you, yet I do……
You have a heart and a soul. You are a stranger,
but are you really? As what's so "strange" about wanting love
and wanting to be loved?

You are outside my inner circle
yet I can *feel* your humanness since the blood
that flows through my veins is also your life source

Your name may be a mystery
but your dreams, your hope and wishes
are *so* familiar to me

You hurt like I hurt, you need like I do
You want the best for your family, just the same as me
I may not know the inner-most workings of your mind, but I
Know you think of future goals and a brighter tomorrow.

We may not be blood relations; we may not run in the same circles
we may not live in the same zip code but we share the *same* race; the *human* race,
and we live in the human community.

Your tastes may differ from mine; your likes may even be my dislikes
but at the end of the day, when the proverbial numbers get "crunched,"
and all that can be done, gets done, the truth of the matter is….
although I *don't* really know you, in fact….I *really* do….

Just DO It!!

Without being morbid and dwelling on the obvious; we have but a short time in the physical realm. Yet we sit in our comfort zones and we hug them so tightly that success finds it hard to squeeze its way through to get to us. We allow years to pass us by, as we waste time thinking of the years we would have to take to either train for a profession we *really* want, write a book, learn to play a musical instrument, or learn a new language.

However, whether we do the things we want to do or not, the time WILL pass anyway, and when the years have passed, you will look back and say if only I had taken the plunge, then today I would be what I *always* wanted to be and doing what I *really* want to do. Time *will* pass whether you are using it to *fulfill* a dream, to succeed, and not just operate from a place where you are here so therefore you *accept* your situation for what it is; ignoring all the pointers to another path; that path that will make your life worthwhile.

If you are thinking of something you *really* want to do; to scuba dive, to bungee jump, to learn to salsa dance, to do sign language, to mountain climb, to adopt a child, to *finally* sing at karaoke, to volunteer; *whatever* it is, *do it now*!!. For as surely as you are alive today and can think of what you *want* to do in the future, it's just as clear that you don't have *forever* to wait to do it, as our days *are* numbered.

Happy "doing" folks as it's in the *actual* doing what you *want* to do in this transient life that you will discover your *reason for being*....

Reflective Directions

Looking in that mirror, staring straight into eyes afraid to look back at the real you. Shying away from half-truths and untold lies, wrapped in a mind that's living in denial. Cracked mirrors showing distorted parts of a life smashed but not completely broken - leaving second chances looking right back at you *challenging* you to look back.

Smeared lenses, blurry irises, blood-shot eyes spelling unclear glances of iffy directions, to paths you need to take. Reflections of time past - that had nothing to do with future plans. Visions of a path that should have been direct but which ended up crooked by virtue of the means you used to transport yourself from surety to uncertainty.

Retrace your steps, change course, chart a new path with a re-programmed compass that points you to new avenues and broader lanes that allow for better negotiation away from those hurdles that are smack in the middle of the road of your life.

Reflective directions….looking back at those "wrong" directions, but only as landmarks that will help to highlight paths never to be taken again….

Changing the COLOUR of your REALITY....

I have found that it is when I am at my **worse** emotionally that I *learn* how *resourceful* I can be in formulating *solutions* to move myself from a space I do not want to be in - to someplace where I am immersed in *contentment*!!.

It is indeed a *choice* to either *stay* where you are or to *rise* above your issues and see the *brighter* side of your situation. When you *change* your way of thinking, your reality will change to fit the colour you want your life to take on. You see, life will not always give us all that's rosy and wonderful. If it did, then it would have to be named something else, since life is imperfect and we exist in essence in the dual reality of good and bad.

But if we store enough of the goodness that is inside and around us, then we will have the reserve we need when we have to dig *deep* to chase the blues away and create the kaleidoscope of different resources that we need to not just survive but also to *strive* in a world that sometimes threaten to cast grey shadows over what we would prefer to be our constant rainbow-coloured existence.

Even though it cannot always be bright and sunny from where you sit, you can decide what colour glasses to peer through. Choose clear lenses so you can properly see your way through to the other side of what ails you.

Unturned PAGES....

Spaces of "iffy" thoughts - of what would and could be
drafts with empty spaces waiting to be filled so you can turn the page
opportunities untouched
places unvisited
lines left off and places skipped
I's not dotted and T's not crossed
as you hesitate to move into the unknown.
Going back to make unnecessary corrections
changing things that are already perfect....

erasing
changing
re-arranging
endeavouring to stay on the same page – but….
the story continues and we get to –

interesting places
long-awaited spaces
endless possibilities
unwritten scripts
ready-to-read lines
and the end of a story that you know you will like.

Go ahead, turn over that other leaf in your book of life
and discover the storyline of that next exciting chapter....

Another Day Means Yet Another Opportunity

Just waking up and seeing the rising of the sun of a new day is a blessing; a privilege. It spells an opportunity to do something we put off doing yesterday; to fulfill a dream, to make a wrong right. It affords us another chance to pick up from where we left off, and to do what we have been dragging our feet on doing.

Today is **the** day, tomorrow is always a maybe. So **grasp today**, embrace it, and treat it as if it is your last day. Your days ARE numbered, and you may never get the opportunity to do what you want to do if you allow today and the opportunities it brings with it to pass you by.

If you have been chaffing to do something in particular that you keep putting off for tomorrow, make *today* that tomorrow, and go forth and *do* , *be*, *act*, *live*. *Today* is *your* opportunity to shine, to grow, to achieve. to love, and to believe that you *can,* as today is your opportunity to stop waiting to live and just start *living!!*.

RENEWAL

I awoke one morning with a sense of I am so not ready to face today, after going to sleep just hours earlier feeling both emotionally and physically drained.

But the dawn afforded me *renewal* and *light* at the end of my cloudy tunnel.
The sunlight that peers through my window panes as soon as it rises from behind the cloud that obscures its light in the night time, signals to me that it's an opportunity to reach into my inner me and pull out the light that is *always* there, no matter how dim it may seem sometimes.

As I meditated on the rays of sunlight I can see shining through my window, it made my heart *glad*; glad that it is *still* beating – each beat signaling another chance to make wrongs, right, take another path, and to keep hope alive.

Sadness and loss are a part of life, but the sunlight that shines through my window but went unnoticed before, served that morning as an emblem of the recurring fact that *every day* we lived to see, is one that gives us a *wonderful*, *enchanting* opportunity for a *refreshing* of our heart, spirit, soul and mind; and it should remind us that renewal is *always* possible, even in spite of.…

You and I, Equals US....

We come into this world as blank slates; all fresh and shiny and new, and ready to be 'written on.' How we turn out has so very much to do with who writes on our brand new slates, what is written on that slate, and what we allow to stick, as well as what we learn to delete. It is so very necessary to delete those things that are negative, and that would otherwise leave scars and blotches that could prove permanent if we are not careful.

Prejudice and hatred are not inherent, we were not born hating each other, or thinking we are better than the next person. Those were things that were written on our slates by those whose responsibility it was to nurture, teach and to guide us in the right way.

Is it innate in us to be selfish, to be all for ourselves, to think only of self, and everybody else is just rungs on a ladder that we climb to get to where we are going? Are we *really* supposed to be our brothers' keepers, or is it that we are supposed to take what we can from this life and from the people around us, make our lives as good as we can make it, then take our exit, having gotten as much as we can; not caring about what our lives meant to, and what we could have done for others?

Why were we born into families, why do we cultivate friendships, and care about our co-workers and church brethren? Is it that we WERE in fact born to share, to care, to be about *us* and not just *me*?. We are all brothers and sisters of the human race. We may not all share the same human blood type, or share the same DNA, but if God is truly our father, then we cannot help but be related.

So I ask, where is the caring for others, where is the empathy? To what end do we love our stuff and ourselves so much that we forget to love each other? How can one mother love her own flesh and blood so much, but can turn a blind eye to another mother's child who she sees is losing their way?

When we have come to the end of this journey we call life, what would we have accomplished outside of having high-paying jobs, nice cars, a bigger house than the "Jones", more gadgets than we can use, more money than we can spend? Will that be all we have to show as our "claim to fame?" would that be a life lived to its fullest; one lived to be an example, to be there for someone who needed you?

In the grand scheme of things, if all we do as we pass through this temporary thing that is life - is to live only for ourselves and those in our immediate circle, then what have we contributed to mankind, to the "us" that you and I make up in this world? If our love and our caring are only big enough to be extended to those we call our relatives and friends, what of the rest of mankind, of our brothers and sisters that were all also created by our heavenly father?

As I sit in my own little corner of what is such a vast universe, I resolve *today* to spend the rest of my natural life being kinder, more caring, more sharing, more understanding, more giving and more opened to seeing those around me as not just a mass of human beings, but as *individuals* with hearts and souls, and feelings, and *needs*, and hopes and dreams: Mere mortals like myself whose lives and existence could be lifted or changed by just a smile or a kind word or *simply* a willingness to listen. This could save a life, cheer a soul and make someone's life just that *little bit better*, and sometimes that's *really all it takes*.

Chapter 3

Hopes, Dreams and Peace of Mind

"Un-cloud the steps of your destiny by living your dreams and holding onto hope as the lifeline to your journey to peace of mind. The sky is merely the beginning of where your dreams can take you, but you can go even one better by following up on your dreams and making your reality as awesome as your dreams. It is almost impossible not to realize a pursued dream. Dream big, dream often but never merely dream; ALWAYS remember to LIVE your dreams" (MC).

Beginnings

I look upon the *vast world* before me just waiting now to engulf me in the *newness* of borders I am yet to cross. I *excite* at the thought of the horizons yet to be shown to me, the nooks and crannies I am yet to *explore*. I smile at the thought of *new countries* I will see, the *new cultures* I will experience, the new *smells*, and *tastes*, the new *places* I will lay my head to sleep.

I relish the thought of new novels to read, new sentences to build, *new memories to form*, new lessons to learn and new "shoes" - literal and otherwise to fill. I wait with bated breath for what is around corners unseen, avenues yet walked, dreams yet to come true, visions to be realized and missions to be accomplished.

I salivate at the thought of what will happen next; where will it lead me, what the *outcomes* of my *new ventures* will be. It sends chills up my spine to think of the *exciting* and *thrilling* adventures that lay just a step ahead, waiting for me to sprint to catch up.

I *embrace* these *beginnings* with *all* that's in me, as I look forward to my visions becoming reality, and my dreams coming true. I invite *the unknown* to make itself known, the not yet discovered to reveal itself to me, and the soon to be, to become.

I am *so* looking forward to my beginnings, what about you?

Circling the Rainbow

Intertwined *colours* or pure beauty

placed together perfectly to reflect a promise so dear –

in a place that it can never be missed

at a time when you cannot but remember why the promise was made.

The out-of-this-world smiles etched on faces that look upon this wonder,

those gleeful eyes glued to beauty undefined and untouched by man's hand -

half circles of the completion of an assurance that lasts *forever*,

a promise that can *never* be broken.

Incomplete circles *absolute* in its trinity of *hope*, *faith* and *trust* –

that tomorrow will indeed be a better day;

a day wrapped up in a package of wishes

that's transcended to thoughts that *dreams* can still be realized

and promises are not just for fools…..

Infinite Possibilities

Wide-opened skies
spaces untouched
races to be won
love to make
friends to meet
history to write
orgasms
laughter
fun
truths to find
philosophies to sprout
hearts to touch
Music to make
thoughts to share
ideas to formulate
lips to kiss
hugs
sensation
feelings
euphoria
hearts to race with excitement
smiles to give
flirts to receive
companionable silence
attuned thoughts
chemistry
QUIVERING BODIES
exotic dreams
ECSTASY
curled toes
LOVE
peace
contentment

Battles to win
others to cheer
life to LIVE
oceans to cross
cultures to experience
minds to mold
personalities to learn
happiness to embrace
hands to hold
lives to touch
people to meet
joy to seek
lessons to learn
fears to conquer
giving
receiving
touching
bad habits to lose
new ideas to share
knowledge to glean
views to impart
thesis to prove
dissertations to defend
SEX
shopping
FOOD
talking
evil to conquer
goodness to spread
wild abandonment
TRAILS TO BLAZE....

the POSSIBILITIES are ENDLESS!!!!.

Cross Roads

Is it the **years** at your place of employment that determines whether or not it is time to **move on?** For me, the years are not the determinant for moving on. **The feeling of not being fulfilled**, and being completely **bored** should be what **propel** you from a space of mediocrity to a place where you know you are occupying your purpose.

Funny thing is though, we are **creatures of habit**, and we like to inhabit our **comfort zones** for long periods of time, even when those comfort zones has become somewhat uncomfortable. **Fear of change**, as well as fear of the unknown and of risks, often keeps us where we are, and hold us back from realizing our **true/full potential.**

The world like they say, is your oyster, and your intention should be to eat it **all** up. If the truth is to be told though, I too am scared of the **unknown**, but I use the adrenaline that accompanies fear as a motivator of change instead of a deterrent. Fear should not dissuade you either, especially not from adjusting your present reality **if it is no longer the reality you want**.

When one era has come to its **natural end**, stop holding on simply because it is what you are accustomed to, but prepare yourself to **embrace something new** as you look with **excitement** to the fact that the **future** can be whatever **you** want it to be.

Are you at a cross road? If yes, are you **ready** and willing to **actually** walk across the divide of the world you are presently in - to inhabit the other one that is waiting for you? Take the walk, as out there lies a big universe with **countless possibilities** waiting just for you on **the other side.**

Just Because....

We sometimes do things with an *ulterior motive*
even if we do not admit to ourselves that is what we are doing.

We **trust** if we are trusted
We *like* someone if they like us first
We give to get something in return

We think before we act, not to make sure it is safe to do so
but many times just to be *sure* as to how our actions will benefit us.

In the face of it there is nothing wrong with being cautious and looking out for numero
uno - especially in a world where "*only the strong survives*" and if you do *not* look out for
you then who will — but, have you ever done anything in your life *just because*;

you *should*
you prefer to
you are *happy* to
you always wanted to?

Can you *love* someone just for love's sake - with no need for security, money, someone to
"have your back" or anything else "up your sleeve"?

Can you allow yourself to *like* someone just for who they are
Can you *trust* someone just because they *deserve* to be trusted
and not wait for them to trust you first?

Tell someone *you love them* today, just because…. they *deserve* to be loved,
　　　　trust someone just because…. they have *proven to be trustworthy*.

Free yourself to give up your cynicism, as even if *life's experiences* have made you bitter
and dis-trusting, it is up to you to *choose* to treat people how they deserve to be treated;
on the strength of who they are as individuals and not as a collective whole.
　　Let go and live today, just because….

"Endings"

The **ending** of certain aspects of your life points you to **the gateway of a bigger, more exciting path** for you to **embrace** and to conquer.

We often see the end of a job, a friendship, a love-affair – as the worst thing that could **ever** happen to us. But when we have come to the end of that part of our journey, we have now been freed to concentrate our energies on being receptive to the other, more important things and people life has in store for you.

Spend the time in between what you are leaving behind (that which has served its purpose) and what you are about to embark on - to **re-group**, and to mentally, spiritually and emotionally prepare yourself to begin again….as you recite to your inner you that….I have run the race and that course is now done. I am ready for the new beginnings that are awaiting me….

New horizons, new challenges, new dreams to take me to terrains unknown. I am now ready to conquer something new, to be victorious over something else, to pursue avenues that will make life worthwhile, and to positively declare, **beginnings here I come!!**.

Dream Stealers

Stomped beneath feet of envy
crushed in the dust of uncertainty
hidden beneath the fear of risks
clouded by unbelief
delayed by insecurities
dragged in the mud of I don't know
diluted by delay
weakened by doubts
broken by fear
stolen from your too loose grasps
failed due to lack of trial
stopped before it ever even got started
stalled by hesitation
re-arranged and constrained
killed by spite
torn to pieces by the lies perpetuated by nay-sayers
derailed by inaction
re-routed to "never-land"
shoved to the back-burners of your plans
conveniently forgotten
exchanged for a watered-down version;
substituted for something that doesn't even compare
pushed back on the agenda
shuffled around on your calendar -
black-out dates
forgotten appointments
neglected todays
unused tomorrows

A cocktail of all the afore-mentioned- mixed in with **procrastination**, and yet **another** dream is gone....maybe **forever**....but you can always turn it around if your dreams are....

taken from under destructive feet
removed from uncertainty to "this is definitely what I want"
revealed from beneath unfounded fears
buoyed by belief
lived instead of merely wished for
pushed forward by excitement
strengthened by courage
made whole by determination
held tightly in your confident grip
displayed instead of hidden away and
free to evolve into its full potential

A dream realized is one given wings to fly by a spirit that is prepared to not merely dream, but to *live* the dreams you dream......

Peace of Mind – Aint No Thing Like It

In a **hectic** world where sometimes there is **no place to hide**; no space to **rejuvenate**. Even when you are afforded the physical sphere in which to do so, your mental and emotional space is so crowded that you struggle to find the quietude amidst the chaos that swirls around and inside – so loudly, that it drowns out any form of hush and contentment.

You have to work so hard for the fortitude and the drive to muscle through it all, in an effort to grab and hold onto and that which makes you **happy**, and **calm**, and **joyous**, and **peaceful** and clear

p – aths that lead you to

e-verything you've ever dreamed of

a – chieving even in a life of

c-onstraints , as you collect **all** the calm you **possibly** can

e-specially for those days when you can use it **most**

Be transported to a place where all is calm, where life's ups and downs are placed in their correct perspectives and where the downs are taken in strides and the ups are embraced for what they are, and held onto for as long as humanly possible.

Peace of mind….one of life's most **priceless** gifts that we would pay almost **any amount** to obtain but that can only be attained when we consciously decide to live life to the fullest, leaving behind the worry over things we cannot change.

Tranquility

Journeying to a place inside wherein amity lives -
a corner of your mind where all's well and everything is just fine.
The meadow, the hammock, cool sea breeze -
a space of contentment; worries are all on freeze.
Half-closed eyes, deep soul-stirring sighs-
a wisp of Jasmine, a taste of apple pie.

Rolled-up jeans, wave-covered feet, toes crinkled by wet sand -
strands of classical music, fish tanks and sun-kissed cheeks.
Writing lines, humming familiar tunes -
occupying a head-space filled with romance and full moons.

Broad smiles of genuine mirth, belly-aching-tears-flowing laughter -
a singing bird, a half-opened tulip. A gardenia, a guitar and a candy-covered strawberry
platter.
A rainbowed sky, a big warm hug, a freezer-cold lemonade mug -
A flirty wink, a toothy grin, a sweet dimple in a baby's chin.

Raindrops on window panes, a walk down memory lane -
A favourite comfy shoe, flowery kisses, silly giggles, yellow butterflies.
The beach, the sky, clean sheets and lemonade -
long glasses of almost-virgin pina coladas,
cheesecake, roots reggae, a baby's joyful coo.

A cool pool on a warm summer's day, thoughts of sweet, special memories.

A mellow mood, exotic food, a picnic under a shady tree -
freedom to roam, hot chocolate with foam - all set the stage from
complete tranquility....

Chapter 4
Determination, Joy, Freedom and You

My evolution as a being of the human race is taking me to places where I am beginning to appreciate the things I do have, and worry less about those I aspire to obtain. I seek to be happy in my now, as I work to achieve the dreams of my tomorrows. You are the master of you own destiny, be fueled by your many blessings and see life as a continuum; you were born and therefore you must transcend this realm, but in the interim, live your life to the fullest, determined to be happy and free throughout the journey (MC).

Finding the Happiness Within....

I have **run** through the "meadow" of *despair*

trotted through the vines and thick shrubbery of the forest of *darkness*

have plunged head first through the wilderness of never-ending inner struggles

strolled over life's broken glass barefoot and purposeful,

prepared to bleed my way to something I knew just *had* to be there....

I have walked through *heartache* willingly; convincing myself that was the path that

would lead me to where I *must* be.

I have sprinted quickly in *many* different directions at the *same* time, in my effort to escape my own reality in its present state, simply because I wanted no part of the path it was pointing me to.

My denial was so much *stronger* than I admitted it to be, as I *shut* my ears and my *heart* to what *really* was. So....

I've looked under rocks

turned over "new leaves"

peered furtively behind opaque curtains,

and stared *intensely* at *firmly* closed doors *willing* them to open.

I have dug deep into holes in the middle of the sinking sands of life,

in places where the *holes get re-filled* as soon as they are emptied

I have *kicked* persistently against immovable walls

shouldered my way through seemingly impenetrable crowds

and fought my way into depths of mystery and sometimes even misery

as I *searched*....

a search that has taken me *up* the valley, *down* the creek, *behind* the shed, *around* the road, beside the alley, *into the dark of night*, and beside waters that were not at all still.

But....as I turned my look *inside* myself, I *finally* found that which I have *searched* so *long* for.... the *happiness* that has *always* lain *within!!*.

Wishful Thinking?

Is it too much to ask for *kindness*?

Is it ridiculous to *believe* in others?

Is it just too inconceivable to think that we *can -*

do unto others as we would have them *do unto us*?

Am I just too way off-base to expect *caring*?

Am I incredibly naive to hope for *peace* among *all* human kind?

am to ambitious to think that *love* will win out over hate?

Why do I *still* hope for *compassion*, hope, caring and the realization of *dreams*?

Is it *all* just wishful thinking?

I PRAY to GOD not!!!!

Being True To You

Lies, facades, *pretending to be what you're not*
Masks, shadows, *hiding who you truly are*
Cover-ups of massive proportions designed to *taint the truth*
and add colour to your *falsehood.*

Half-truths that make things look so much better than they really are. White lies to divert attention from insecurities and smoke screens perfectly placed so they obscure flaws you want no one to see. Lies of omission, only answering what is asked, when the unsaid is so much more important.

Furtive glances, fear to show what you perceive as weakness.
Loud laughter, broad smiles, *personal bravado,*
hidden pain, muted emotions, telling yourself everything's alright.
Telling *me* the lies, sprouting untruths to *self.*

But to what end, when admitting to a fear, a weakness, a flaw, a failure - sends it out in there to a space in the universe that is just waiting to accept it and spin it in your favour?

Why tell yourself you're happy when you're not, when that wasted energy could be used to *actually* make yourself happy? Why fake an orgasm, force a smile, deprive yourself of a good cry?

Be *true* to the I that is *you*, release your thoughts and feelings -
making them available to your own honest evaluation; no matter how messy,
since self-truth is the *only* route you can take in setting yourself *free!!*.

Because I'm Here....

i'll lend a piece of my heart to a **cause**

i'll listen to someone's woes

i'll talk to someone who wants to hear a voice other than the one in their own head

i'll hurt

i'll cry

i'll hate

but i'll also….

laugh

and

love

and

rejoice and then….

i'll explore my options and shoot for the impossible

i'll explode in ecstasy and purr in content

i'll breathe in deeply; the smell of life and exhale in wonderment of **all** there is to **see** and

hear and **feel**….

i'll fight

and fail

and fall

but i'll also….

succeed

and **revel** in my hard-won victories as I **absorb** the experiences of every

molecule of each **second** I am on this planet.

Because i'm **here**……

I'll LIVE!!.

Self-love

I am *me*, I *love* being me, would have had to be *born* again if I wasn't *Marvette Camille.* If you don't love you, then who can you love? You *have* to first love *you* before you can love another.

I am *fearfully* and *wonderfully* made as I was made in the image of the master carver. I love my eyes, my lips, my nails, my hips. I love my gait, my eloquence, my feistiness, my fearlessness, my ability to own a room when I walk into it.

I love my extremeness; my being *both* tough and a big ole' softy at the same time; love that I can sit with kings, and with garbage men, and *still* have a whale of a time with either or.

You *have to* love *you* in order to be able to extend love to those around you. Self-obsession to the exclusion of others, their feelings, thoughts and desires is *not* a good thing, but *loving* yourself for who you *were created to be* is imperative, as it is *only* in loving *you*, that you can *truly* love those around you.

Self-love rocks - I LOVE ME SOME ME!!.

Forevermore?

Does *anything* lasts *forever*?
does love, does hate, does sorrow?

Does *anything* go on *indefinitely*?
does hurt, does anger, does disappointment, does ecstasy?

Does *anything* hurt for **always**?
does a broken heart, does failure, does rejection?

Does *anything* linger for *infinity*?
does a broken dream, does misunderstanding, does the
effects of unfairness and injustice?

Thankfully some things *do* fade, and some even *completely* disappear after a while.
But *yes*, some things *do* last, go on *indefinitely,* and linger for infinity.
True love does, *real friends* do, so does the peace afforded us *only* by our creator, as
does *genuineness and truth*

For *those* I would *gladly* do………. *forevermore*……..

Newness

It seeps over you with its *delicious* freshness
grabbing your attention and HOLDING it

It makes you all warm and fuzzy
all tingly and bubbly and bright

It puts a pep in your step, a spring in your gait
a smile on your lips and hope in your heart

It excites and terrifies
it brings anticipation, wonderment and fear

It makes you *anxious* to see tomorrow
while you STILL look forward to the rest of today

It delights you
It entices you
and moves you

It makes you smile those secret, *knowing* smiles
and laugh those head-thrown-back, shoulder-shaking, belly-cramping laughs

It tickles and caresses, it *purifies* and *refreshes*
It **pervades** your thoughts and *captures* your imagination

Find the newness in your every day existence; not just seeing each day as just another day,
but as something new to look forward to, to learn, to *enjoy!!.*

Lighten Up

Can you **laugh at you** - do you see the humour in all the silliness that surrounds you - even that of your own making? We have a choice....life **is** what it is, but more often than not, it is **truly** what **we** make it.

If we spend half of our lives **crying over life's inevitabilities** like sickness, disappointment and death, and then turn around and spend the next half of it dwelling on our mistakes, our failures and all the rest of it, then when do we get the **time to enjoy the wonderful things that life has to offer?**

Lighten up on you for a change; laugh with/at life, since the choice **really** is yours. Either you get up every day crying over the spilt milk in your experience, or you try to find **the lighter side** of what you are going through.

When next you come upon some **divergence** in your plans, some **hitch** in your usually smooth path, some **hindrance** to your way forward - step over, under or around it; and even if you stub a toe or break a nail, roll an eye and shake your head if you must, but whatever you do; **you just have to lighten up!!.**

Whatever you experience today, use it as a **building block**; that rung that **propels** you into your next experiences that are in tandem to make you better for what you have to face come tomorrow. **Laugh a little** at yourself, at life's quirks and at God's wry sense of humour. You'll find that it makes life and its ups and down **so much easier to take**. After all, there **is** in fact a time and place for **everything** under the sun, so do not leave your radar stuck on the doom and gloom when there is **so** much that is **bright and light** all around you!!.

Cry, scream, rage, kick something if you must, but after you have done all that; **please lighten up!!.**

Release Yourself For <u>Your</u> Blessings

The **creator** and the **universe** are **vast** and **powerful** enough to **bless** us **all**, but we have to be ready to receive our blessings. We sometimes fail to remember that **what is meant for us cannot go to someone else.** But are you **ready** to receive **your** blessings and will you **recognize** when it's knocking at your door? Sometimes our lives are so **over-shadowed** by all that is happening to and around us that we are neither **prepared** nor **equipped** to receive **our blessings**.

We tend sometimes to waste our precious energy on **<u>harbouring</u>** **_envy_** in our hearts for the blessings others receive, when there is so much for us all, so much so that even if our "cup" is overflowing with blessings, we **still** could never use up all that's **wonderful** in the universe. Take the very next second to **channel your energies into a receptive mode** so you will be free of anything that could sully the path to what you are due.

The path swept clear of unnecessary debris is always more favourable to those blessings swirling all around you. So be ye **always** alert and prepared to receive them by placing yourself directly in their path, and by letting go of past hurt and disappointment, thereby **untangling** yourself from the chains of "what ifs" and "if onlys" and grab a hold of "this is my time to receive the blessings meant for me." **_Leave a path wide opened to what is rightfully yours so you not only receive your blessings but also own them!_**

Embracing <u>Your</u> Joy

From the day we were **born,** we were destined to **die.** That was **so** not the original plan of the creator; but the creatures muddled the script and therefore our realty has changed and now we are faced with the cycle of life. So since we know that **life is transient,** then we should be **cognizant** of the fact that no plans we make, no riches we hoard, no material things we cherish, and no amount of trying to "freeze-frame" our age and existence will change the **inevitable.**

As such, while we are here it is **imperative** for us to **grab** what happiness we can. So tell me, are you happy being **an academic**, working in the job you are presently employed in? Do you spend all your waking hours and even some the sleeping ones trying to manically acquire those things you think will make you happy if you possess them; be it money, success, clothes, shoes, women, men, **power?**

Are the dreams you are "realizing," **your** dreams, or are they the dreams of your significant others; parents, siblings, spouse or friends? Is your expected joy derived from what **conventions** and **expectations** have **dictated** that you follow?

Are you **joyful** in what **you** have accomplished? **Do you experience pure, unadulterated joy** when you step outside of yourself and face the mirror that is your life? Are you doing what **you** want to do, have **always** wanted to do, have always planned on doing?

If the joy you **should be experiencing** is non-existent, then you are helping the universe and its inhabitants to **steal your joy.** Do what makes **you** joyful, that makes you smile and sigh the sigh of the contented, the satiated and the satisfied. This can **only** happen when you find not what brings joy to others if you live your life to please them, but when you have finally found....**your joy!**.

Freedom

I'm on **cruise control**
gearing down
slowing down
getting ready to apply those brakes

I'm on **auto pilot**
i'm there because I have to be
just doing the bare minimum
that is required of me

I am at the **slow down light**
getting up to the red light
waiting to shift another gear
to go in another direction

The end is right there
I can't touch it but I sure can see it
and **feel** it, and sense it

I can't wait for the **ultimate release** the end will bring
the **freedom** to "do" and **be** me,
I have already shifted to the **next** gear
my **next** direction is being plotted

There wasnt any stopping me before
but it is even more so now since for **all** intents and purpose
I
AM
FREE….

It's Moving on Time....

Stuff happens, tough stuff, rough stuff, hard stuff!!!!
Things happen, *really* terrible things that leave you *reeling,* your head spinning, and you
feeling.... like it's about time to give in, pack it up, and listen to the fat lady's song.

Life *kicks* us in the shin, *punches* us in the stomach
knock the wind out of our sails, push the chair from under our asses
It slaps us, tears our hair out, and "rain on our parade"....

Leaving us tired and fed up; about to give in and give up,
to throw in the towel, be down for the count, shrug our shoulders and say *enough*!!!!
It pushes us so *close to the edge* that we have to hang on for dear life so as not to fall into
unseen *pitfalls* just waiting to swallow us up
It beats us down so much that we have to *fight* to dig ourselves out of the *ditch*.

But do we *give in* or *give up*?
We can't, we shouldn't, we mustn't!!
We take the stink and spin it into something sweet,
or if the stench is too much for you to stand,
then step over it, walk around it, or *use* it as its own step ladder to get beyond it.

Leave all the baggage behind, smack it, wrap it, snap it shut
and then throw the key away, only to be retrieved if you need a reminder as to where you
are coming from – 'cause if you lived through it, you can push through it, and if you
push through it, you can overcome it.

It's MOVING ON TIME....

The Significance of You

We sometimes doubt our own worth and purpose on this earth and question why here, why now, why this. We "if" and "but" and "maybe" as to just how *important* we are. We search in *abstract* places, and *unnecessary* spaces, when our *worth* is right there in the essence of who we *are.*

Our definition of ourselves is too often derived from external forces and erroneous sources that present us with a picture that is nowhere near the truth of what is in us, of us *is* us. Your value should *always* be determined by you and *never* by others since try as they might, and no matter how well they think they know you, no one, I repeat, *no one* knows you as well as you know yourself.

You fight to fit in and be a part of something else in order to feel like you are worth something. But your worth should be measured against the idea that there is *no one else in the world that is quite like you* and that you were created specifically to fit into a place in the world that no one else can fill. Keep reminding yourself of your vast importance to the universe and that *you are not here by accident but rather by design.*

Pay homage to your own significance by living a life that reflects your knowledge of just how *precious* you are to yourself, to others and to the *universe.* Always remember to never forget that h**ow much you are *worth* is largely *contingent* on how much *worth* you place on *yourself*!!**

****Inspired by Denise Antoinette Simpson; after having a conversation with her, I was deeply moved by something she said and it gave birth to this piece. Be mindful of what you say and to whom, as you never know who you may be inspiring or hurting for that matter****

Chapter 5

Conquering Life and its REALITIES

"No one promised us a life devoid of difficulties but when you are going through our "go through" use it as an opportunity to reflect on the best tools to cope with your difficulties. Use the hard times to GROW and think of them as RUNGS in your journey that exists so you can GREATER appreciate the WONDERFUL things life has in store. LIVE, LOVE, GROW and REMEMBER to make EVERYDAY your BEST day ever"!! (MC).

Life Unscripted

No lines
No actors
No rehearsal
No call backs
No auditions
No agents
No "take two"
No scripts
No do overs
No directors
No curtain calls
No repeat performance
No applause
No encores
Change of roles and
No casting calls

Instead there are;
Conversations
Real people
Opportunities to learn
Second chances
Changes
Successes
Triumph and
A discovery of self

Life does sometimes imitate art and vice versa, but the reality that is life – far surpasses anything art could ever conjure up, even from its deepest imaginings. The **reality** of life is simply that life **is** its own reality and there is **nothing** that can substitute for it. Enjoy life for what it is, as it **is** the most precious gift you will **ever** be given.

Sometimes I Wonder...

Your personal transience tend to stare you blatantly in the face when someone you know, but especially someone you love dies. And when they die at an age or in a way you believe to be too young or to be too "untimely," it brings thoughts to the forefront of your mind that may have either not been there at all, or were pushed way back to some place you very rarely visit.

I wonder sometimes what there is to life if after all is said and done, you acquire all the "this and thats" in the entire universe, if they don't make your time on this planet a happy one? We procure stuff, and hoard them like squirrels do, we get degrees so we can feel as if we're self-actualizing, and becoming what we "ought to" become "optimally". But personally, I have discovered a few things in my time here on earth. Like a man chasing a woman, acquiring things in life is all in the chase. Then these things more or less lose their appeal after they are conquered.

Everything I have ever thought I ***needed*** or would "simply die if I didnt get" have lost their appeal in such less time than I ever could have imagined they would. Whether it was the VCR back in the day, the digital camera in more recent times; the first class honours that I would have felt like I had failed undergraduate school if I hadn't gotten, the trip to Africa, the first car and on and on. It was in the "getting to" all those things that I found the joy and the excitement. This is because life is ***not just about stuff***!!.

It makes me realize then that life is so much more than that. I wonder though, if it were possible for me to, after I transcend this realm, look back at my own life, what would that overview of the time I have spent here be? Would I see a happy person, a person that did the things she ***wanted*** to do, not just the things I either felt I ***should*** or ***had*** to do. Would I see that the things I did were more than just for a fleeting high that left me flat afterwards, and simply yearning for something; ***anything*** to make the time I spent here at least worthwhile - the next high perhaps?

I think as of now that I will ***only*** do those things I ***want*** to do, that will make me happy and fulfilled, because I certainly, for the time I have left, wish ***not*** to be a slave to expectations and conventions, but instead, find ***my*** niche in this life, instead of what I think I should be doing. Then, at the end of the day, even if I wont be able to do the overview of my life from the" great beyond," I would still have felt that I fulfilled ***my*** purpose on this earth, ***whatever*** that purpose may be.

Do ***you*** wonder sometimes? You ***should***....

Life's Journeys

In the grand scheme of things, Whatever is happening in your life at a particular point in time is that which is salient to you and what feels like life's greatest occurrence *ever*. We sometimes take itsy bitsy things and blow them up so big that they become larger than life, when in truth and in fact, they are oftentimes (especially when measured against other things that follow them in your lifetime), just those "small stuff" that we need not lend so much energy to. However, what is important to you is just that... what is important to you. It may seem silly to others, but *own* your feelings anyway, be true to *you*, and embrace your experiences no matter how trivial they may seem to others.

Life's journey is personal, it belongs to you and you alone. You may share aspects of it with family members, friends and even acquaintances, but at the end of the day, it's YOUR journey. The paths you take, life's ups and downs, the kicks you get in your butt that leave you feeling like you will NEVER be able to get back up again. The joys, the pleasures, *all* the experiences are a part of this journey we call *life....*

When you look back on all the twists and turns that this journey takes you through and will continue to take you through until its time to transition from here to "there" let it be a look of "that was a part of the journey" and not one of "that shoudnt have been." Growth should be experienced as we move from one place of our journey to another, and once we have learnt from our experiences; good and not too good, then they should not be seen as "mistakes", but rather as rungs of the ladder propelling us through our journey.

Life is short, unpredictable and fleeting: *live, laugh, love*, like there is no tomorrow. After all, more often than not, we dont have the privilege of knowing when this part of the journey will end. So while you have the opportunity to live, let's go about the business of living with *everything* in us.

Enjoy the journey, it is *short*, but gosh darn it, we *do* have a say in whether or not it is *sweet*!!.

There'll be Days like this my Mama Said....

There are days when all seem lost and the dawn doesn't come with the refreshing and renewal that it should.

....when it feels like it makes no sense to roll out of bed and face another day that is reminiscent of other days gone by

.... when you do roll yourself reluctantly out of bed, move around like a robot on auto-pilot, and live simply because you are already here

....when no matter what you do, nothing seems to change, and all your prayers and tears seem to fall on deaf ears and stony ground.

Those "blue" days when the sun is shining, and the birds are singing but you don't see nor hear them

....when **all** your problems seem insurmountable and insoluble, no matter how **hard** you work at trying to solve them

....when the music has lost its luster and the song in your head is like a recurring dream that no longer brings a smile to your face or peace to the inner you

....when the smile passes your lips but is **nowhere** near your eyes, when your laughter is nothing but sound with **no** merriment

....when the tears that used to cleanse you and make you feel whole again, only serve to redden your eyes and make them swollen, but has none of that "cleansing agent" it is supposed to have

....when your feet are so heavy you just want to give in to that need to sit or lay down for days on end and exist instead of living

....when life's ups and downs seem heavier than they usually would feel on another day, in another space, in another time

....when everyone and everything seem so far away, or otherwise of no use to you and your troubles.

Mama *did* say there would be days like this. But when these days do present themselves, just *know* that "this" is just for a matter of time and that you *do* have the fortitude to *overcome*, and to come out the other side *stronger* for it. Tomorrow looms, and with it comes another day that brings with it *much needed hope,* and *another* chance to fight our demons, battle our adversities, tackle our issues and *win!!.*

The Void

The space you left is forever vacant as no one else could fill it
your physical aura has disappeared this realm. Your laughter has been silenced,
your tight, warm hugs are no more, except for in my imaginings, and remembering….

I can't pick a phone up and hear your voice at the other end
the voicemail on your phone isnt even there anymore
the long heart-to-hearts, sharing dreams, hopes and aspirations
still happen on my end, only I dont hear you responding to me….

Although you're not here in the physical, your spirit lives with me **forever**
As the way you touched my life and my heart can *never* be taken away,
not even by the finality of *death*. You are gone from me, and my arms can't hug you,
I can no longer hear your voice, but there is *one* place that is *forever* filled with you -
cause there will *never* be a void in the space you occupy in my *heart!!*.

For everyone who ever lost someone….fill the *void* with *precious memories*….

(Dedicated to my Mama Joycelyn Myrna Facey and my Brother-Friend Albert (Al) Plummer).

The Muted Voices of the Down-trodden

How do you not **HEAR** me when I am **SCREAMING** at the top of my lungs til i'm hoarse; **RIGHT** there in your ear drum????. Yet....my pleas go unnoticed, my cries for help unheeded, and my expressed **NEEDS** unsatisfied - *I AM HUMAN!!!!*.

Do you **NOT** see me????

I am **RIGHT THERE** in front of you

Don't you get that blood flows through my veins

and a heart beats within my chest? - *I AM HUMAN!!!!*

Why won't you **ACKNOWLEDGE** my presence???????

am I just too lowly for you, is my lack of affluence an affront to your **VERY** existence?

I AM HUMAN!!!!.

Why do you **DELIBERATELY** turn your back on my cries for help, when you **CAN** offer me a helping hand? Am I **ANY** less human than your neighbour, your friends, your **CHILDREN**, your **FAMILY??** - *I AM HUMAN!!!!*. I lay **BARE** and **NAKED** before you, with all my **PRIDE** and **VULNERABILITIES** there for all to see, but yet you **STARE** right through me as if am not even there. Well I **AM** here, I have RIGHTS, I FEEL, and HURT and NEED, JUST like YOU do. *I AM HUMAN GOD DAMN IT!!!!*.

Please HEAR me, SEE me, as if you DONT, then it is almost **INEVITABLE** that I will be among the things that go THUMP in the night that spells HORROR, DESTRUCTION and maybe even DEATH for you, your loved ones and the PRECIOUS worldly possessions that you hold so DEAR; even to the utter DETRIMENT OF YOUR FELLOWMEN!!!!.

  ACKNOWLEDGE my existence I **BEG** of thee, as I **DIDN'T** ask to be here, yet here I stand, **BEGGING** you to validate my **HUMANNESS** and return my **POWER** and **RIGHTS**, as POWERLESSNESS leaves me feeling VULNERABLE, and vulnerability makes me feel WEAK and WEAKNESS pushes me to fight for ACKNOWLEDGMENT.

PLEASE SEE ME I BEG OF YOU, or my INVISIBILITY will manifest itself into something so *GROTESQUE* that you will have *NO* choice but to….

LOOK

AT

ME!!.

The Facade

Your face is showing the opposite of what your heart is feeling
You smile, and even laugh when you are DYING inside
You come across as tough when a wind blowing from the wrong angle
would knock you over flat on your butt

You strut your stuff when you wanna crawl somewhere and hide
Your "toughness" is your defense against the big bad world
The facade is your armour both for body and soul - as you wiggle behind shades
and hide beneath veneers. You do the "ostrich" with your head beneath the sand, and your
"hiney" stuck high in the air - exposing the very secrets you are trying to conceal from the
world.

Why not just be *you*,
Why not just be *true* to you?
Even if the whole world cannot accept you for who you are,
lying to yourself is the *biggest* lie there is.

While you don't need to show the world your all, hiding who you *truly* are, especially from
you, is like being a walking dead. Be *you* no matter what, and the *truth* you will find when
you step out from behind the facade will *free* you to receive the *blessings* that are in store
for you. Then the world will have *little* choice, if not to love you, then most certainly to
respect you for being true to yourself.

"Fashion Show"

It's more than just a fashion show; where your make-up needs to pop, your outfit needs to rock and your hair has to be stylin'. It surpasses mere rollin' in the finest wheels, chillin' on the hippest strip, having the largest number of chicks, shelling out the greens, and having the biggest entourage.

It's a little deeper than the who's who, a lot more serious than drinking the most expensive booze and it encompasses more than just your bling, your "thing," your partying and your hanging at that spot where you know you are more likely to be seen.

Hey you, and you, yes you **and** you, life was **never** meant to be ***all about you***!!. By all means -wear your poppin' make-up, rock your fashionable outfits, style your hair, roll in your fine wheels, chill on the hip strip date the "fillies" spend the dough, hang with the bros, drink the Hennessey and pop the champagne, bling out and profile.

But spend some time figuring out what else is there to life; it's also about true love, family, friends, giving back and paying it forward. Giving of yourself - with no expectation of getting something in return, searching for and finding your purpose and carrying it out with a view to making not just self but also making others happy.

Life's no fashion show, but you can still make it beautiful by giving something back to the universe and leaving it even better than you found it.

Heartbreak

No thread is strong enough to fit back together, those pieces thrown about and scattered asunder on thorny rocks that bounce into waters so deep you cannot find them. The needle is useless except to create more puncture wounds in a place that is already porous and bleeding. You stare at the broken pieces at your feet and wonder if it's possible to ever re-assemble them, but then you think aint **no** super-glue strong enough.

Pain so deep it's hard to even breathe, as tears as thick as blood - stains your face, as they stream hotly down cheeks tender and bruised from so much weeping. You cannot think without your heart contracting and giving birth to acid oxygen as you fight for your next breath. Ribcage so tight you feel your heart being forced from your chest and then left to be trampled on by wild horses in a stampede designed to bury you alive.

Tears are unstoppable and the thought of loving again seems impossible as you're hemorrhaging from pores you didn't even know existed. Drained of seemingly all your life's blood you force yourself to stay alive, as you fight to stave away those feelings of dying a slow torturous death from a pain that's just too much to bear. Lost interest in usual joys, lost joy in usual interests; straining to do the things you once loved.

Bird songs no longer so sweet
sunsets losing most of its luster
black skies
blue songs
red eyes
sands shifting
earth shattering
destiny shaken
innocence lost
….as you face your intense heartache

Life has sucked from you - your vim and stolen the pep in your step, but you shuffle your way back from your lowest of low, scrape together your heart's pieces and exhale the unbearable pain that pervades that thing that occupies the space where your heart once was.

"Heart closed til further notice" and "do not enter signs" are prominently hung. "Don't even breathe the same air im breathing" looks are being rammed down throats and "stay the **hell** away from me" stares are etched semi-permanently on a frowning face that has almost forgotten how to smile.

But you bend down to pick up those pieces, as you take a single step back to reclaiming your heart and reminding yourself that broken or not; the heart still beats and life is still sweet even though now it's mixed with a touch of cynicism and tainted with a smidgen of caution of things concerning the heart.

You breathe just a tad easier as your chest expands from its contracted state back to its normal size to re-accommodate a heart now working normally; and even though you don't know it yet, and can scarcely even imagine it, inside you lies a heart that will soon be ready.... to love again.

Home Away From Home

Unconsciously conscious of the soft noise around you as your sleeping brain registers sub-conscious feelings of peace you're forced to have. White lights above you, mind blurred from "eye-closers" filling a body lying down and vulnerable to strange eyes attached to gentle hands.

Knowledge and know-how coupled with grace and mercy as heavenly hands work with earthly wisdom to remove alien matter from painful insides. On needles with v's that starts with I's, in beds that are made for one. Quiet nights with lots to think about, and weak moments of fear and doubt.

Vulnerabilities staring you straight in the face - with bold clear eyes of unblinking rigidity, as they remind you of your morality. Slow-moving steps as you walk your way back to health and count the days getting back to your own bed. Sweet helpers dressed in white with smiles of encouragement, who gently wipe away run-away tears of a heart overwhelmed with helplessness. Familiar faces bringing reminder of the outside world with their presence and laughter muted by stitches that threaten to burst.

Saying goodbye to a place we go to be born and sometimes to die and that keeps us alive somewhere in between. Then welcoming the place wherein lives those things that make you sigh - a pillow, a smell, a face, a feel. Back on feet that are a little more steady and armed with the consciousness of the wonderful frailty of that precious thing we call life. A journey not yet finished, with **so much** more life left to live, as thankfulness takes the place of a mind pretending not to worry....

(Written after a three-day stint in the hospital after yet another successful surgery; another reason why I celebrate life every day I live to see....)

"Stay-cation"

My body's here but my mind is FREE to roam, my soul to sour and my heart to explore - the wonders of the world that is beyond the physical confinements of where I presently sit.

I'm not shackled by my physical inability to do as I please, when I please - as my mind is *way* stronger than my body's need to be somewhere else - and has *long* scaled the walls of my limitations of the physical kind and have reached and held captive; mind food of higher degrees than usually reached, soul satisfaction that *many* never experience, and heart-contentment that will *never* be realized by those who *desperately* seek it, even though they are physically free.

I am temporarily "grounded" by my circumstance but *permanently moved* in my spirit to make a difference in the world I inhabit, to be that who contributes to my space in the universe in a positive way - to give light and air and love and *peace* to those I encounter, even from behind bars of human constructs.

STAY-CATION, my temporary physical space where I re-group and grow - where I extend the expanses of my mind, stretch to its *very* limit, the *depth* of my soul as I *find* the *me* that is *within* me, and give my *heart* the circumference it *needs* to propel me to be in touch with *all of me....*

**** *Inspired by someone special to me who is incarcerated in a physical prison but who is freer than many people I know, and dedicated to Mark "Buju Banton" Myrie, whose grace even in spite of his present struggles, has mirrored the strength of character that will no doubt motivate others to make the best of whatever life and the universe places before them.****

Those Forever Goodbyes......

They have **no** foreseeable end as they **drag** so **painfully** along paths so dark and forlorn. They **stain** your existence with long tentacles that wrap around you in **sadness** and *despair* as you *struggle* to dismiss them even temporarily.

Their *stench* leaves you *stunned* as you *fight* to hold your breath while *recoiling* from the *powerful* smell of *permanent* loss. Will it *ever* end - is there a light at the end of a tunnel so *dark* you can *taste* it?

Why goodbye when hellos are so much sweeter; when having and holding those dear to you - near to you, makes life *so much easier*? They say absence makes the heart grow fonder, but what say they, when that absence has put asunder, the ones you love, *forever*?.

You spend an *eternity* with these *never-ending* so-longs as you try to let go of the past and look towards the future. But they hang on with such *tenacity* that they become an extension of your *heart and soul*.

They *clutch* at your insides and *squeeze* from your core, *all* those feelings you try to bury *deep* beneath a safety net of self-preservation, while you *fight* to keep unwanted feelings at bay so you can *survive* from day to day. They are your *constant*, your *ever-present* - even when relegated to the *deepest* recesses of your mind.

When the heart's *ache* is *unbearable*, the memories are most *precious* and time seems to stand still....ohhhh those FOREVER goodbyes........

*** death is the continuum of birth and life, but it hurts so very much to lose those we love to death's finality. Cherish those you love, so your forever goodbyes will be tempered with priceless memories***

My Brother's Keeper?

Sometimes we get so caught up in our own stuff that we swear the world revolves around us, and that no one else matters, or that they exist just to feed *our* need. Are we our brother's keeper?

You "woe is me" and think of our next "fix" be it food, sex, the *must have* pair of shoes, the "*can't live without it*" piece of jewelry, while someone *right* next to you is hurting; a hurt that if you spent one second away from the mirror of your own life, you'd see in that person's eyes – that *need* for even one minute of your time to stop and pay attention to their need. Are you your brother's keeper?

We are filled with our own importance, and are way too busy to lend a helping hand, or give an ear to someone else's issues. We scoff at the weaknesses of others as we laud our strengths and achievements over them. Are we our brother's keeper?

When you neglect your neighbourly duty and instead play with your gadgets, and live in your own little world of "*me, me, me, me*" while others all around you are just waiting for a kind word or a good deed, just to survive *one more day*. Are you your brother's keeper?

Admittedly, I *am* guilty of *all* this and so I *know* that many times I have *not* been my brother's keeper. So do I wait on December 31st to make some abstract resolution that will be forgotten by mid- January, or do I get up and start *being* my brother's keeper *here and now*? I *am supposed to be* my brother's keeper and as of *this* day, I will *act* like it…. *Will you??*

The "Dark Room"

I sit here "*developing*" the strength of my mind as I recoil from the *pain* that lies within me. My tears are all spent as it just hurts *way* too much for them to fall from eyes swollen from tears past.

 Food does not entice me, making love enters not my list of needs but instead my *heart* cries out for something to fill a space that is outside merely just a particular body part. The pictures in my head are blurred with my un-shed tears as I grapple with the meaning and feelings of time filled with SO much heartache that I sometimes wonder how I manage to even live through it.

Music doesn't cheer me, hugs don't presently warm me like they used to, but instead they leave me *cold* and needing something *more*. My *deep-seated* feelings of hurt are *fully* developed as my heart hurt something *awful*; a pain that is *in-explicable* but is as *real* as the next breath I am about to take.

Breathing doesn't make me feel alive; it's merely an automated function of a body that is weary from a mind that has had no real respite from sorrow. *Laughter* doesnt lessen the pain that is lodged in my throat that is making it ever so *hard to breathe*!!.

I hear the click-clicking of my internal *camera* as it pictorially *recalls* the old feelings and mix them with the new ones as I *struggle* to keep my head above it all so I can make even a *semblance* of sense of the *whys* that are reverberating over and over in my *room of darkness*. *Kisses* don't stir me and *tears* don't relieve me of the *gloom* that hovers over the space I occupy inside *myself*

One fine day I *will* be able to *step* out of this *dark room* that threatens to completely envelope and suffocate me. I *pray* that day will be *today*.....

**Do you suffer from depression? If yes, it is nothing to be ashamed of. We have all been there at one juncture or other of our journey when life kicks us around as if we were footballs and leaves us feeling as if all has been lost. Acknowledge your feelings and then seek the help you need to set you back on the path to a happier you.*

Living in a S.C.R.E.A.M

It's always so loud all around you; the *intense* noise that's inside, that's outside, that surrounds and saturates you in the depths of its *greedy* grasp. You try to shut your ears to it, to drown it out with positive thoughts and deep sessions of introspection...but it persists.

The high-pitch sounds of the "un-quiet," those deafening shrills of "louditide" and "confusism" that leaves you *breathless* with the *need* for peace and quiet.

You fight to escape its sharp tentacles that are so penetrative that not even head-phones can keep the outside noises at bay, and no amount of self-talk or positive meditation is able to mitigate against the loudness that is on the inside.

You are living a *scream*, but you ache for that intermittent silence that serves to bring soothing to the soul, peace to the spirit, calm to your existence and *threatens* your threshold to tolerate and endure all the noise that surrounds you.

You are living a scream, but you *deserve* some degree of peace, so search hard to find it, even if it means you have to *create* it for yourself, as it is imperative that you preserve some *you* time, some *down* time, and some *quiet* time to enjoy life.

Turn down the noise, tune out the unnecessary, but whatever you do, step away from the noise even long enough to breathe....

................R .e .m .n .a .n .t .s................

I lie here exposed and vulnerable

my "insides" opened and bare for ALL and sundry to see

My life spilt over and running down the gutters of "where-so-ever-will,"

with destinations unknown, and routes "un-plotted"

I stand there right in the path of those laser beams that see *right through me* and leave me chafing to cover my face so no one can recognize my *exposed* parts and sit in the squalor of my own private shame – wallowing in the nakedness of my *troubled* thoughts and deeds; that even though not out there for all to be party to, seem *highlighted* in neon signs beckoning *greedy* eyes to swallow them up inside their *bottomless* depths

As I shake off the *residue* of my *brokenness*, I turn a *complete* 360 degrees; *trampling* on the *negativity* of the past, the soot of the present, and the uncertainty of the future, as I gently *mold* my *remnants* into what is now the *best* of what's left of me….

If You're Among The Living, Then L I V E!!

Your heart is beating; you are able to see, hear, smell, taste and feel all that surrounds you. You are capable of loving, caring, empathy, and sympathy. Blood rushes to your head, heart and loins when you see the person you love. You cry when you miss someone and laugh and experience glee, when you are in the presence of people or things that you enjoy.

This means you are **here** - you are **alive**. So since you are among the living then **live**!!.Stop waiting for the "next shoe to drop" the next "axe to grind" the other "ship to sail," while life passes you by, and you lose time you can **never** get back.

Refuse to live your life with regrets that keep you laden down with things you **cannot** change and instead, start taking control of your own existence by taking on what you **can** control and using it to your benefit. Quit bellyaching about the things you do not have, and be thankful for and concentrate on the things you **do** have - **life**, **health**, **family** and **friends**!!. Stop putting off your living for another day, suspending your life for **only** when it's easy to live. Exchange your "i'll do it tomorrows" for "let me fit it in today".

If you're feeling your heart beat against your chest, if you're breathing and aware of what is happening around you, if you are able to see, hear, smell, taste and feel all that surrounds you, then you **are** obviously among the living, and therefore it's about time for you to **live**!!.

Liquid Me

I can feel my emotions overtake me as I wipe my **tears** for the hundredth time and seep through myself into a feeling of weakness that gratefully promises to whisk me away from sadness so thick I can cut it with a knife.

I am boneless as I wait for pain so intense to wash over me and leave me breathless from its cruel force, and I pray for relief and release and respite from my present consciousness. I would welcome sleep, a temporary coma, or amnesia, *whichever* comes first.

My mind's legs are so wobbly that they scarce can hold me up, as I ponder why ME, why HERE, why now, why *ever?* I *struggle* to keep my thoughts steady as they leave me shaking from fighting to keep them at bay for as long as I possibly can.

I am drifting with that tide that goes nowhere in particular, but everywhere at once, as I melt into feelings SO deep that I am almost lost in them. I am floating, soaring, melting, drained of all that's in me...for right now, I am merely the *liquefied* version of me…. That me that is *broken* but waiting for that release for a soul *strangled* by a pain so *debilitating* that you have to fight to get out from under it.

I sigh a sigh of relief that frees me from the pain that has held me captive, as I look for and find the restoration that always lies behind *every* last tear I have ever cried,

The Need To Bleed......

When you have gotten to that place where old wounds are festering and are left to marinate in their own juices of regret, neglect, disappointment and unfulfilled dreams. When life stinks of dissatisfaction, of failure, of unexpressed feelings and unrequited love; and has a stench of self-loathing, lack of love for self, depression, a paucity of hope, and the need for redemption of the human spirit.

After you've been through all of that, then its now time to release yourself from the residual effects of all you've been through. Flush from your system, all that has been keeping you back and clogging your insides, preventing you from breathing freely and receiving the blessings that are rightfully yours.

Then it's time to bleed from your inner columns - all that which festers and reeks, and that leaves you in an utterly devastating state of brokenness and defeat. Bleed so that old wounds are healed and gaping gashes can finally be stitched up on your way back to wholeness.

Do you feel the need to bleed?.

Locked Upppp....

Feet cemented to a ground covered in unfruitful soil that sets in motion non-growth and stalemates with nowhere to go. Hands tied behind backs with handcuffs of denial and dead-end thoughts leading down a path to places devoid of light and colour.

Mind clouded with unfortunate thoughts taking me to horizons bereft of optimism and ending between closed spaces that threaten to completely squeeze from me my brain matter of positivity.

Heart unopened with its keys buried beneath rubbles of uncertainty and disquiet. Forming avenues of sadness that is being pumped to vital organs, creating a path of bloody bile that gets stuck in my heart's throat seemingly forever.

Release me, let me go to free my feet, my hands, my mind, my heart - to walk, to clap, to think, to feel; feelings of freedom, of being unshackled, and the ability to roam free, in my body, mind and soul as right now i'm so locked up that my mind's eyes are unable to see beyond their self-created walls.

I am now ready to take back my freedom and show life who is boss. I *was* locked up, but I have fought to *untangle* myself from the bowels of a self-inflicted prison and now I give myself permission to set myself free.

Feelings

What do you do with something that is *so* powerful that you can feel it, but is so elusive that you cannot touch it? When you heart hurts so much it is like a *physical* pain, but it is not something you can actually touch so as to pluck it out of your life and throw it away? What do you do when a feeling takes over all that you *know*, *think* and *do*? but you can't actually remove that feeling no matter how hard you try?

Do you have the power to divert your feelings from the path they are taking or do you make it a habit of suppressing them until they resurface another time, in another way to create havoc in your life? Is the term "owning your feelings" always good advice? Does owning them mean you *have* to suffer through them, or is there is a way to work around them and to *not* feel?

What do you do when you own those feelings and then they are so overwhelming you can barely stand the stress of it all? How does one feel the feeling that they are feeling, and then move on to a place where that feeling does not affect you anymore?

Feelings are what they are, and if you're not feeling it means you are *not* living. The happy, orgasmic, proud, wonderful feelings we embrace, but the terrible, sad, depressing ones we try to avoid as they hurt so much. But allowing yourself to feel the feeling you are feeling when you are feeling them give them validation and enable you to deal with them as they come so they don't cause *unnecessary* issues in the future.

Acknowledge your feelings and *own* them, as that will help with the process of achieving *closure* on your path to *healing*.

Standing Up To Life

You were *crippled* by your past
shackled by your regrets
pinned down by your history
and *tied down* by your baggage

You are physically free, but you allow life's stuff to make you a *prisoner* of your own circumstances. You are able to stand on your own two feet, but your *unwillingness* to *let go* of the past has made you a candidate for life's wheelchair.

You are *restricted* by your own *narrow-mindedness*
handcuffed to your own inflexibility to *change*
constrained by things you have *no* control over
and *restricted* by the invisible *chains* on your feet

You can *walk* but you are *manacled* by your *obsession* to *always* look back instead of forward. You can *run* and *jump* but you remain *stagnant* because it was *easier* to do, and you are *confined* to your old way of thinking that no longer works for you.

Impeded by your bad habit of *closing* your eyes to the obvious
encumbered by the universe's negativity that you take onto yourself *knowingly*
and *obstructed* from achieving your goals by your *tendency* to simply roll over and die.

Stop allowing life to *obstruct your vision*, hinder your dreams, thwart your *future plans* and *prevent* you from *truly* living. *Bust* out of that emblematic wheelchair that is *merely* a conjuration in a mind that is actively sabotaging your own success. *Step away* from *negativity* and *flow* with the tides that are pushing you to *live your destiny*!!.

"Checking In"

When you have done *introspecting*; finished that inward look, *evaluated* that space you are in that you have always wanted to move away from, then it is definitely time to check back into the business of *living*.

When you have exhaled, have picked up the broken pieces and have put it all into perspective, then the time has come to check back in with self and with reality as you continue to *evolve* into what you have always *dreamed* of becoming.

When your mind is able to process its need for calm and peace in face of life's chaos, and after your brain has been rested to the point where taking just a few steps no longer leave you completely exhausted, then it is about that time when you *should* re-enter life's fray as you take back that which is your *rightful* place in the space in the universe created *just* for you; that space no one else can occupy.

Take all the time and space you deem *necessary to bounce back* and return to your life that much more ready to continue to live your life the best way it can be lived. Just don't take too long to re-join life, as time *is* of the essence and there is so much more living still left in you to do....

Take A Bow

Life has thrown you around the room;
across the bannister, up the chimney, down a *gazillion* flights of stairs,
over a barrel, through hoops, into the fire, beside *roaring* rivers that you were *forced* to
cross
yet....you are *still* standing.

You have been beaten over the head by life's lessons,
battered by its waves and plummeted by its heartache and pains
but....yet you are *not* defeated.

Your take your licks like a *champion*, brush yourself off and shout *bring it on* to the
next challenge that presents itself. Smiling when you are expected to cry - as you find a
way to laugh in life's face when it believes it has gotten the better of you.

You cry to *rejuvenate* and *refresh* as you wash away disappointment and despair from your
life and welcome *change* to an existence made *new* by a determination to create the kind
of life *you* want to live.

Now take a bow, accept the applause, graciously soak up the standing ovations that should
come with your successes, even if they only come from you. "Pop your collar" in *jubilation*
and be *proud* of the fact that you *overcame* and even in the face of your difficulties you
showcased your *ability* to come through the fire yet *still* came out on the other side better
than you were before.

Go ahead, *do it* - take that bow for conquering life - you *so* deserve it!!.

Chapter 6

Learning From Life's Imperfections

"You are perfectly imperfect. Confront the world and its troubles as a victor, as your attitude is TRULY what will determine the outcome of your days. When you accept the fact that you are PERFECTLY fine even with your OWN imperfections and that which exists around you, you are less pressured to live up to what is accepted as being "perfect." Perfection is ONLY achieved if in its achievement it makes you HAPPY" (MC).

LIFE

Its mysteries may **never** be unraveled: The winding roads of sorrow, the steep hills of hardship and pain. Those spirals, dips and sudden turns that leave contours and indentations on slippery paths throughout the journey that all come together to make life what it is.

The good, the not so good and even the horrible all work together to make it worth living. We **rejoice** in the happier times and learn to **rise** again from the trenches of failure, heartache, disappointment and all the other ills we have encountered and learn that we are stronger than we thought we were.

As you maneuver the hurdles, the shifting sands beneath your feet, those crushing lows, the shallow ditches of fleeting happiness, and come upon those **exhilarating** highs and plateaus of ecstasy, you inevitably come to the realization that life is **truly** worth all you have had to endure as you work your way through the **living** of it!!.

Imperfections

They are **everywhere**, some visible, some the figment of our own imaginations, some we choose to only see in others even though their headlights are glaring in us. But as I sit up to acknowledge my very own imperfections, I come to the realization that they are simply another layer of the me that is me.

They set me apart; they render me unique;

That mark on your leg, that spot on your cheek, the indentations in your thighs, the difference in the sizes of your breasts and eyes. The unsteady gait, the jerky, uncertain movements of your dance technique, your cracked tooth, that toe that neighbours the big one that is just a wee bit taller, the tiny hole in the middle of your hand, that mole on your nose, your tendency to giggle when you are nervous, or the inability to sit still for too long.

These are the things that separate you from the crowd, that make you - you, make you memorable and not just merely one of the "pack." So, instead of seeing them as liabilities, view them through new lenses that will illuminate them and give them the reflection of the assets they can be if you simply look at them with fresh eyes and a new attitude of acceptance, reminding yourself that you are **perfectly imperfect**.

Don't Sell Yourself Short

You are a child of *the KING*, not a King, but *the* King, which means you are *special* and if anyone tells you differently, then they are *lying!!*.

Being royalty means then that there are certain things you *should not* take from others, for instance, if a man treats you as if you're his personal slave, his punching bag, and the means through which he feels like a "man", then you are *not* being treated in the way you *should* be treated.

If a woman treats you like an emotional *money machine*, where she comes *only* to withdraw but *never* to lodge, and never acknowledge or validate your feelings as a man, if her favourite thing to do is to emasculate you and put your testicles in a little glass somewhere so she can look at them all the time like a trophy, then you *must* realize that this is a woman who is *no* good for you.

Do you have a child who has come of age, but who *refuses* to take responsibility for his/her life, because you have *made* yourself their *permanent* bank account? Do they treat you like *crap* otherwise; no phone calls on your birthday, no visits or gifts on mother's/father's day, but yet is up front and personal, as soon as the credit card YOU gifted them with is maxed out, and the cash you gave them has ran out? If this is the case then in your heart of hearts you *know* that all you are is a cash register, and a mere convenience, then your *royalty* is being trampled on and you're not being treated like you should.

If as a friend, you get a call from that someone *only* when they are in trouble, when they want money to borrow, or a ride to some place, yet when *you* need them for *anything* they are never available, or is never ever in the position to help you no matter how *small* your request, then it's not rocket science that the open door to *that* friendship does not swing **both** ways.

Are you the *only* one at work who is ever willing to switch around your vacation time and days off to accommodate a certain person's funerals, deaths, weddings and births? But nothing you want to do is ever important enough to warrant them changing their plans for you?.

Is there someone in your life where there exists an unspoken "don't call me - i'll call you" arrangement, where *every time* without fail, you ring their digits you get a voicemail, but whenever they call you, you *have* to be available? If someone makes themselves *unavailable* to you, but *expects* you to always be there when they call or come around, then they *are* using you for their convenience, while you on the other hand, does not have such a "luxury."

When you get that "certain feeling" (and you always do), that someone is using, disrespecting, taking you for granted, or taking advantage of you, then they *are*!!.That feeling of your pride, your rights, and your self-respect being taken away from you, and being trampled on, is one you should *never* ignore, as what it means is that you *are* selling yourself short!!.

You were **not** born to be *any one* else's punching bag - be the punches mental, physical, emotional or financial. You are *not* less than anyone else, no matter their profession or possessions. Your feelings are *valid* and *important*, and should *always* be treated as such.

If for any reason your power to choose and to be treated with the respect you know you deserve has been taken away from you; *take it back* by *deciding* to no longer be treated the way you have been treated in the past. No child, no man, no woman, no friend, no co-worker - *no one* is worth you selling yourself short for, as *God indeed made you special*, and it is now time for you to take back the you - you *know* you *should* be!!.

Uncertainties

Where am I?
am I either going or coming
am I where I should be?

Is this the path I am meant to trod
are my feet planted on the way that will take me forward
or are they loosely placed on grounds that are ambiguous and iffy; not going anywhere in
particular?

Who am I really?
am I true to myself
is what I do and say what I mean to
or is it all a facade so that my insecurities,
my vulnerabilities and my fears are hidden and I am protected?

Where am I headed?
am I walking the straight and narrow
going into paths unknown and downright scary
or am I headed for paths that I deem to be safe and sure?

What do I want to become?
am I there already, am I half way there; just a quarter of the way
am I working towards it or just thinking about it and wishing for it to be?

Will I ever be the me I want to be?
will I self-actualize or will my self-actualization be hindered by the ifs and buts I put in
my own way
will I refuse to battle my demons and thereby thwart my own future endeavours?

What about you?
where are you?
who are you really?
where are you headed?
what do you want to become?
will you ever be the you - you want to be?

The uncertainties of life will always exist, but there also exists - surety, control and permanence. If we take the bull by the horns and steer our lives into the directions of our dreams, then the uncertainties become our sureties and our ifs and maybes become our *yes* and *sure*!!. Uncertainties can hinder your growth and development but only if we refuse to take the risks necessary to overcome them and create what is for ourselves, *our* certainties!!!!.

When You Know You Miss Someone

I have come to learn that the people who are important to me aren't important because of what they can offer me in terms of material things, but for who they are, their aura, their spirit, their companionship, and my ability to reach out to them just to hear their voice and to be in their presence, and I am cheered and made to feel so much better, despite what is ailing me.

You know you MISS someone:

When there is no one else who can fill that void, when everything you do, hear, taste, feel, think and even imagine reminds you of them.

When you ache because you can no longer share what you usually shared, that unique "thing" that makes something that much more special.

When your days are just that little less brighter, and your laugh though still joyful and happy is underlined with just a little hint of sadness.

When your down-times are filled with bittersweet memories and your up times are touched with regret that they are not there to share it with you.

When holidays are still happy and welcomed, but yet are dreaded, when good times could be better, and bad times seem so much worse.

When the pure joy you would otherwise feel is slightly coloured by unease for being so happy even though the one you're missing is not there.

When you smile and mean it, but the mirth still doesnt reach all the way to your eyes. When you laugh so loud it hurts, yet there is still this hallow space inside that the laughter cannot fill.

When everything around you is just that little less sweet; the chirping of the birds, that song on the radio, the movie on the "tube".

When you are happy, yet sad, celebrating yet hesitant to do so, seeing everything through different eyes, enjoying life to its fullest yet is conscious that there is still something missing.

When life moves on its merry way, but you're still somehow lagging behind and holding on to memories for dear life. When you're in a crowd, and even surrounded by other loved ones, yet you are lonely for that one special person.

When life is the same yet **completely** different, and time albeit passing by, but standing still. When life as you know it has changed **forever** because that someone is not around: This is how you **know** you really miss someone.

It's ok to miss the people in your life that you love but are no longer around, but make sure you embrace them while they are still here, and love them like crazy while you still can in the physical realm, as cliché' as this is, tomorrow **really** isn't promised to **any** of us.

Smoke Screens

Lies, facades, *pretending* to be who you are *not*. *Masks*, shadows, hiding who you *truly* are from eyes that pry but also from those who merely want to *see*..

Cover-ups of massive proportions designed to taint the *truth* and credence to your *falsehood. Half-truths* that make things look better than they *really* are; *white lies* that divert attention from *insecurities* and smoke screens perfectly placed so they *obscure* flaws you want *no one* - not even *you* to see.

Lies of omission - only answering what is asked even though what is left *unsaid* is so much more important.

Moving on the *sly*, furtive glancces to see who is seeing you mixed in with the *fear* to show what you perceive as being weakness. Loud laughter, broad smiles all in pretend *bravado.* Hidden pain, *muted* emotions - telling yourself *everything's* alright.

Sprouting *untruths* to self - but to what end, when *admitting* to your fear of weakness, a flaw, a failure - sends it out there in the *universe* to *unseen* but *tested and tried* powers that are just waiting to *accept* it and spin it into something *powerful*?

Why tell yourself that you're *happy* when you're not - when that *wasted* energy could be channeled into *making* yourself *gleeful?* Why *fake* an orgasm even of the *mental* kind, force a smile, and even *deprive* yourself of a good cry when the release it would afford you would alter your state of mind?

Be *true* to you - *release* your thoughts and feelings; *availing* them to *honest* self-appraisal, since *honesty* to self is the *only* truth that will *set you free.*

Excess Baggage

You *struggle* under the weight of it all, and is left feeling as if your feet are **laden** with dried cement, rendering you unable to move. You are suspended in time like a ship with its anchor firmly set in the sea's core, swaying constantly but going nowhere fast.

You are ***stuck in the past***, unable to really live in the present while your future mocks you from its high perch where you are able to see it, but unable to put it into perspective.

The ***choke-hold*** it has on you leaves you no real room to navigate your way through what is necessary to maximize your efforts to live life your to its ***optimum***.

But if you shoulder your way through the cobwebs that they form around your life, and ***chisel*** yourself out of the encasement they create, then the possibilities for growth, love and the ability to elevate yourself from beneath your baggage overload - is ***endless***!!.

Shed the excess baggage of negativity, self-hate, doubt and fear, and use the space it frees up to add those things to your life that will make life worth living.

After All is Said and Done

After we have **killed** each other for material gains, trampled on a few heads in our race to reach the top of the ladder and when the "crab in the barrel" mentality has gotten us **nowhere**, what next?

After we have achieved **all** those things we thought would make us **joyful** if only we could attain them, after the money is made, the houses and cars are bought, after all the "bling -bling" and the "profiling," and when we have **exhausted** the attention of our "audience" who is no longer looking, what then?

After your manhood has been satiated by your **many** conquests, and you have been vindicated by your women's lib and after you have proven how learned, eloquent, intelligent and affluent you are, then what?

Whatever it is that you think you just **have to have**, that you **need**, that you **are**, if when you lay your head down in the middle of the night, you are **unable** to sleep because of a **heavy** conscience, a **sad** heart, a **restless** mind, or a **tormented** spirit; when you pass a mirror you are **unable** to stop and take a **good** look at yourself without feeling like a **failure**, despite all that you **have or own or think you are**, then in the grand scheme of things, what have you **really** achieved?

If you end up financially poorer than you planned, have one less degree than you would have liked, have a less expensive car, and less shiny stuff than you dreamed, but find that you **smile more, laugh louder, feel more contented, step lighter, love harder more, sleep in peace at nights and ultimately leave a legacy of decency and honour**; and have attained **peace of mind,** then **that** is what **really** matters...... after all is **said** and **done**!!

"If Only" ....

....the sweet smell of the rain was never tainted by the ruining of the atmosphere

....neighbours still cared for each other as they did in times past

....kids remained kids instead of forced-ripe adults in little children's bodies

.... politicians were after something other than just the need for power

....the masses was interested in anything other than just today's satisfaction

....the learned would share their knowledge instead of lauding it over others

....the preacher man would be convicted by his own sermons and start loving his neighbor as himself

....the carpenter would take care of his own home the way he does other peoples'

....we would take the time in traffic to introspect and pray instead of honking our horns and cursing

.... we could embrace what we have now instead of worrying about what we should have

.... we loved each other's children as we love our own

....the mistakes of yesterday would be the lessons of tomorrow

....those living uptown would stop looking down their noses at those down-town

.... those down-town would stop envying the up-town

.... the downtrodden would be lifted up and the exalted would be humbled

....the injustices of this world would be turned into fairness and equity

....evil would turn to good and darkness would turn to light

.... love would be given without condition

.... caring for someone else didn't mean they had to have something to offer you

....we would live each day as if it were our last

....the world was the way it was created to be and we didn't destroy our environment

....life was cherished and the feelings of others taken into consideration

*If only.........*then not only would the world be a ***better place***, but we would be much ***happier people.***

Only Human

You rise, you fall, you get pushed, you trip
you land on your butt, You falter, you hesitate,
you second guess your own actions
you are fickle, you are "wishy-washy" and you procrastinate

Your mistakes are many, you even repeat some you already made
You foul up, you trample the paths set out for you and infringe on ones set out for others
You hurt, you get hurt, you offend, you get offended, you fall in and out of love,
sometimes with the wrong persons, and you push away the ones who love and care about
you the most.

You cry, you laugh, you succeed, you fail,
You fall flat on your face, you get embarrassed, and disappointed
You are sad, you're happy, and at times you're even both sad **and** happy; (or what I call
"sad-ppy") as life is serving you **both** sadness and bliss all at once.

To fall, to trip, to falter, foul up, hurt, be hurt, offend, be offended, love, cry, laugh, be
disappointed, be happy, sad, and to err **is** only human.

To **learn** from life's experiences is to be one step closer to **conquering** the down and
maximizing on the **ups** as you try your **darnedest** to survive **yet** another day in your
humanness, is **yet** another **victory** under your belt.

Release

My mind is muddled by life's ups and downs as I try to temper the chaos with the tranquility of all that the **big** hands of my creator has carved out to *inspire* and *calm* in me. My body is tense with the fluster that surrounds it as it *fights* to stay strong enough to take on the daily grind; as I struggle against the fatigue I feel threatening to overtake me.

My thoughts are scattered and wild and centered on too many things at once as I try to rein them in to give them some semblance of a direction; I strain for peace to calm my restive mind. The torment of my soul is palpable as I wrestle with demons real and those created by my very own angst;

but then comes *sweet* release - when I leave it *all* behind to *embrace* that which is *freely* given in a *vast* universe prepared with *everything* I need for *instant* and *constant* peace of mind - spread out before me like a *never-ending* table of a life's "food" as I become the *ultimate* gastronome of love, joy, release and serenity.

My sighs are peppered with sly smiles of contentment, bursts of laughter that emit *pure* glee from the bottomless part of that organ that pumps my life's blood, that beats; that *breaks*, that *loves*.

As I come down from my wave of *orgasmic* harmony of *mind*, *body*, *thoughts* and *soul*; I *welcome* sweet release and hug it *tightly* to my chest with an *unadulterated* sigh of *thanksgiving* as the cycle of life's realities continues......

Life's Lessons

When you went through your "go through" and you look back on the path your life has taken, did you learn?

After you have dissected the mistakes you have made that could have been avoided if only you had taken the time to listen to that inner voice that has **never** steered you wrong, have you grown?

When you think back to the paths you should have taken but didn't due to self-doubt and fear, have you gained a better perspective on who you really are and how your fears can hinder your growth; have you evolved?

After the shit has hit the fan and has plastered its stench all over your life, and has even leaked onto that of others, staining lives in a way that cannot be washed away that easily, has it affected you enough to change your way of looking at things and realizing that what you do has consequences that affect not just you; will you change?

After you have ran out of excuses for your own **foolishness**, and is over accepting the worse from others, and have now come to the realization that you **do** matter, that you **are** important, that what you do, say, and feel **should** mean something and that others **should** give a damn about you, do you **demand** the respect you **deserve** and settle for **nothing** less; have you matured?

If you've been to hell and back, and life hasnt **always** been kind to you, but you just sit back and stagnate in your foul-smelling odours of life, and you keep stubbing the **same** toes on the **same** cracks in your life- street, or you sit in the **same** shitty spots that leaves you stained, then all the **bull** you have been through would have been for **naught**.

However, if you have **gotten up** from the dungeon of your past and **moved on** with **lessons learnt**, grown, **changed for the better**, and have matured and **figured out your worth**, then you have **succeeded** in progressing your existence onto another leg of a ride that will take you to the you – you have always been searching for, and **the best you** – you can ever become.

You <u>Never</u> know....Part l

If you were born, it is inevitable that you *are* going to die
some of us may be "lucky" enough to know how we are going to go
some of us will take our last breath while laughing, making love, singing, driving
but the bottom line is – it is inevitable.

We hope and pray that particular sicknesses don't get us
We pray that the gunman's bullet is marked for someone else
We turn our noses up at others who have been stricken by something we deem
to be beneath us or that we are *immune* to.

We negate their "humanness" because they have some disease or other
We neglect them and shun them and scorn them. We think this can *never* be me
but you *never* know since you can't predict what is going to happen in your future and
what may afflict you and ultimately take you out. You never know when you will be in a
position where you will *need* someone to be in *your* corner.

When you *shun* someone because of their afflictions; because of the hand life has dealt
them, just *remember* that tomorrow is *not* known, it's a mystery, and what it holds for you
may not be something you would wish on even your greatest enemy.

Reach out to someone in need today, not just because of what they can do for you tomorrow,
but simply because they are your *fellowman.* Be kind to others, *lend an helping hand.* All
may be well for you *today*, but as for your tomorrows, you *truly* never know......

You <u>Never</u> Know....Part II

....what someone else is going through, what is in their heart, and soul and mind
the outside may be bright and cheery, the inside dark and dreary.
....what is on someone else's mind, no matter how much they *do* tell you
....what is burdening their hearts that they feel they just *cannot* share
....what is in the *deepest* recesses of their soul that render them unable to
verbalize it.

....how someone else is *really* feeling despite the bright smile on their face
and the seemingly upbeat pep in their step. The heart sometimes is in such pain
that it cannot bear it, the mind is sometimes so clouded with confusion that it scarce can
decipher all that's swirling around, and the soul is sometimes *so* tormented that
the weight of it is almost *too heavy to bear*.

Spend more time listening to your loved ones; "hearing" some of the things they don't say
out loud but are there to be seen in their eyes if you just take a *little extra time to look*.
See beyond their outer coating and look beyond the *surface* to what touches their heart, as
this may just be your chance to save their life....you *really* never know....

**Suicide is one of the most painful ways in which to lose a loved-one. Many times the
signs are there if we just spend a little time out of the everyday grind to pay attention.
If you are having thoughts of suicide yourself, please reach out to someone you can
trust; as sometimes just hearing someone else' perspective on something that seem so
insurmountable to you, is all you need to make it over your problem and come out on
the side of it, alive and still standing**.

Chapter 7

Strength and Triumph

"And when you've done your BEST then you can rest assured that it is WELL DONE, as WHATEVER fruits your BEST bears, it's BETTER than whomever has exceeded YOUR best, if HIS efforts were just mediocre. You are so much stronger than you believe and your ultimate triumph lies in the recognition of this powerful fact" (MC).

Unshackled

Unnecessary weight on already pressured heart valves –
straining to pump its fair share of strength to organs thirsting for new life-blood.
Un-called for stress tied to unknown stressors –
leading purposefully down a path of almost certain destruction.

Untie pesky thoughts and bundle them into heaps of disposable worry;
uproot those deeply planted feelings of unworthiness from a place only you have ready

access to, and *unclog* arteries of life's stagnant bull-crap that threatens to explode into

useless pieces.

An *Unshakable* resolve to clear a trail to life's sweetest destinations – en-route to taking

back what self and the universe stole from you.

"I __Am__ Gonna Do This" – Part I

I was born tough, even, though I have to keep convincing myself of this
My life has forever been mixed with both HARDSHIP and bliss
I get kicked in the teeth by life so often,
that I shudder under the weight of it all.

My lessons are hard learned and are crammed down my throat
so that I can hardly swallow, but i'm too strong to lay down and die
or stay forever in my "stuff" and wallow.
I think God is kinda sorta hard on me because I guess he thinks i'm strong
and I struggle to keep my head above water
but hey, someway, somehow... I *am* gonna do this!!.

If it takes being kicked in the butt,
clawing my way out of the bottom of the bucket
fighting my way from beneath all the *weight* I sometimes get covered under
whatever it takes... I *am* gonna do this!!.

I'm way too smart to fold when life has *so* much more to offer.
I'm much too strong to give in to life's little cruelties and sick sense of humour
It's tough, it's rough, it's a test of my resolve and my "stick-to-it-tive-ness"
But you *best believe* that... I *am* gonna do this!!.

It may take me longer than I planned
be harder than I anticipated
It may go on like what seems like forever
but as long as the sun will rise for me another day
as long as there is *any* way...
then... I *am* gonna do this!!.

Sometimes the *greatest* challenge to my own success is *me*. But since I am smart enough to
recognize my own sabotage be it unintentional then I am *certainly* wise enough to remove
the obstacles from the direct path to where I want to go. But even when it's my "stuff" that
is placed in my own way, come *hell or high water*…. I *am gonna do this!!*.

"I __Am__ Gonna Do This" – Part II

There is **no** block that will have me constantly stumbling
no **humps** in any road **anywhere** that I wont barrel through, squeeze around, or crawl under

If I have to 'weather" the storm, make ends meet and start over from scratch
If I have to take a risk today to create opportunities for the future or
If I have to learn from the licks I take in life and come out on the other side a stronger me

There is NO road too long, no mountain too high, no river too wide
no obstacle that will deter me from the path I want to take

Even if I have to "suck it up" for the time being, and reap the fruits of my labour later on
if the goals I set seem impossible and out of my reach, I will simply forward-think and see the achievement of those goals in my "mind's eye," as I work towards achieving them later.

I will kick and scream, and **fight** and even rebel, but....

whatever it takes, I AM gonna do this!!!!.

As I remind myself today and **every** other day of my **own** inner strength and my ability to pull through **all** the garbage life has already thrown at me from all angles til I sometimes feel as if i'm going under, I also remind my friends and loved ones who are having a hard time at it right now that **you** also have it in **you** to "**do this**", whatever your "this" may be!!

The Hero Within....

The **hero** that **resides** inside of **self** is so much **stronger** than the one you look for outside yourself. Your **inner** you - that **strength** is even **more** than you believe it to be.

Just think back to the **many** times you have **had** to draw on reserves **inside** you that you didn't even **know** existed, and **remind** yourself of how **powerful** it was to **discover** that an hero **does** live within.

When those days present themselves with their ability and their quest to keep you down, reach for that which is always inside you and prove your mettle to yourself once and for all. There is no law that says you **always** have to be strong, but just knowing that you possess that inner strength to draw on when it is truly needed is your passport to facing up to the potholes and wrong turns that will inevitably pop up on your journey through life.

By all means take kindness and respite on offered shoulders when you must, but **always** be mindful of the **fact** that you have the resources inside of you that is necessary to "**save**" yourself not just from things that happen outside yourself, but also from what can sometimes be the most destructive side of you - that lives inside your head and that sometimes seek to sabotage your best efforts to stay positive and to strive.

Be the hero you **seek** and in doing so, you would have **created** that someone you will be able to depend on, no matter what.

Good-bye Yesterday, Hello Today

Your troubles sometimes haunt me and I feel bombarded by your existence. You hang onto me in a tight grip that's choking me to death. But now i'm walking free of you and *taking* my life back. I am forgetting all you did to me, *choosing* only to remember the lessons I have learnt.

I'm shattering the shackles, leaving the pieces behind me and removing the fingers from around my throat so I can breathe again....inhaling the newness of *today*, forgetting the stench of yesterday.

I'm dirtied but not stained by what transpired yesterday, I am bruised but not broken, as I have recovered from the licks I took from yesterday's book, as I go on to live in today. I've learnt from my mistakes, grew from my miss-steps; and I have not been deterred from my dreams simply because of yesterday's ills.

Your purpose has been served, your lessons have long been learnt. Now you're history, as I break free from what used to handcuff me to a time that has already gone down into eternity. You were the bane of my existence but now I will *only* think of you when your *lessons* are *relevant* to me *today*!!.

GOODBYE YESTERDAY.........HELLO TODAY........

I am <u>Not</u> Afraid

To love

To need

To show I care

To let myself feel

To sacrifice

To be vulnerable

To show my feelings

To give a damn

To work hard for what I want

To dream

To wish

To do what makes me happy

To demand what I need for me

To make mistakes on my way to greatness

To start at the bottom in order to work my way to the top

To say *yes* to taking *necessary* risks for future gain

To say an emphatic *no* to anything that makes me uncomfortable

To embrace life with all its ups and downs

To reach out to others in my hour of need

To be there for them in theirs

To believe in myself

To venture into the unknown and to *demand* what I *know* I am worth....

I am *not afraid*, because living a life of fear is *truly* no way to live.

I <u>Never</u> Fold

I am like a ticking time bomb
a raging out-of-control forest fire
a bucking bull
a fast approaching train.
I get a licking and keep on ticking
I am the song that never ends
the pupil that is always dilated
that pain in the butt that never goes away

I am that poker hand that keeps on winning
that song that EVERYBODY'S singing
that energizer bunny that keeps going and going and....
I am the rock that never shrinks
the flower that never fades
the stain that is irremovable

I am *strong*
I am *determined*
I am *unstoppable*
I am *indestructible*....

as even when this mortal body dies, my *spirit* will live on *forever!!*.
You too should cultivate an *indomitable* spirit; one that will sustain you through those
inevitable periods of your life that threaten to get the best of you. Cry if you must,
scream even, but whatever you do, *never* fold your hand of life and make it get the *better*
of you!!.

Redemption

HEY YOU, YES YOU….
Did you overcome *one* obstacle today;
did you *refuse to curl up and die* or run and hide from your responsibilities?

Did you admit to your mistakes
said you were sorry for the wrong you did someone
Did you learn something,
imparted something you learnt?

Were you less stubborn
more receptive
less full of your own importance,
more flexible?

Did you *share* a part of yourself;
given of the part of you that you always thought too special to share
Is the person you are today even *one* step nearer to becoming the person you *want* to
become -
did you *change*?

If you answered *yes* to even *one* of those questions, then *today* you were *redeemed*
Your redemption came either in the form of your *overcoming* some obstacle, *recognizing*
your own strength, *sharing* a part of yourself, being more *receptive* to change, *letting* go
of SELF, and becoming more *opened* to *change*.

Acknowledge your redemption as it speaks to your personal growth and your acceptance
of your ability to *grow* and *evolve*.

Step Outside the Box

Four corners of pure, unadulterated claustrophobia is what that box is; with one side representing a yawn, another serving as the confinement of spontaneity, another a world of utter boredom and yet another depicting the epitome of conformity, stagnation and rigidness.

Boxed into spaces so small that your lungs burn from the lack of sufficient air. Trapped in a space so TINY that you struggle to breathe where there is no room for growth: Mental, spiritual, emotional or creative.

Squeezed inside a space so small that your sense of style and originality gets royally raped and terribly bruised from all the friction of trying to get from betwixt the tight folds of a space that is way too small to accommodate your wriggling about to escape your own confinement, so you can show who you are and what you can do as a creative, exciting individual.

Break away, spill over the lid, bust out from inside those walls of restriction and confinement, find your own niche, embrace your uniqueness and start living in a way that suits you. Move away from sameness, skip around the familiar, remove yourself from what everyone else is into, and carve your own niche….somewhere outside the box….

You Can Rise Above The Darkness

Remove the sheath that is hindering you from *seeing*. Get out from under that *blackness* that is covering you - hindering you from *breathing*. That blackness that is *right* there in front of you, that is *so* thick that you could almost *cut* it with a knife. You can't *see*, but you *know* you *need* your sight to act as your guide as you traverse life's terrains.

Then suddenly your eyes *are* opened, but *still you cannot see*, as your *vision* is *blurred* by your *own* bull-crap, your future is *obscured* by the fallacies of those things you place in your *direct* vision. Your eyes remain *wide-shut* as you stumble *unnecessarily* over feet buckling under the weight of your *very* own obstacles; placed in your way as you unwittingly sabotage our *own* success.

How do you *go forward*, how do you take the baby steps necessary to take yourself out of a darkness that is oftentimes self-inflicted? *Remove* the blinders that *you* created, and *don't* just keep your eyes opened, but *train* them to actually see, to *visualize* and to *understand* what they *are* seeing.

If you are being consumed by perceived darkness, your acknowledgement of this is the *very* first step to *true sight*!!.

You Just Keep Gettin' Up

There must have been or will come a time when the hardships of this life feels like a noose around your neck, choking the *very* life out of you, when the days before you seem oh so long and without purpose; when your pain lasts for such a long time that you wish you could just *disappear* simply to escape it all;

If you are still standing after the very air has been knocked out of you by what feels like a unexpected punch in the stomach, or a swift kick to the groin. If you are still here with all or at least *most* of your mental, physical and emotional faculties still intact. If your head is *still* above water even though you feel like you just want to give in to the persistent currents and just go under, if you are still fighting tooth and nail with everything in your being just to come out the other side of a life that has kicked you around like a ball;

If you have survived something so *huge* that should have had the better of you, that you thought was bigger than you, way above your control. If you have come out on the brighter side of a time *so* dark you couldn't even see your hands if you put them right up to your face. If you're standing when you should have been flat on your back, running if just a short while ago you couldn't even *think* of creeping, singing and giving thanks and praises when you NEVER dreamed you could find even *one* more thing to sing about. If your thoughts are *still* on life and living after going through a period when you wanted no part of the physical realm and you just felt like giving up.

If you have overcome *so* much in your life that when you look back you cannot even *begin* to fathom the path you have trod. If you have been through your "go-through" and you are *still here and still strong* in spite of it all. Then you *know* that giving up is not for you, that your inner strength is such that it won't let you quit, as you *just keep gettin' up*, and you *intend* to stay up, no matter what comes your way, no matter what negatives are thrown at you, set up for you, *you still get up*, and even laugh in the face of adversity; showing it who is boss; then your *strength of character* is surely your *best asset*.

We have all been down in the gutters at some time in our life, but when we *get up*, dust off, *refuel* and set out to *conquer* that which is in our way, then we are able to *move our personal mountains* out of our path, and *remove* that which *threatens* to hold us down and keep us back then we have learnt to *persevere* and to *strive* to always get right back up when life has pushed us down, *as staying down is simply not an option.*

Live Out Loud

Live your life as **loudly** as you possibly can, refusing to be –

a pip squeak
a mouse
a "silent partner"
the wall paper
the fly on the wall
the second fiddle
the foot stool

Instead, be who you are if what you are is someone that prefers to be

Out there
colourful
Outspoken
visible
heard

Life is as **big** as you make it. Make it **stand up and pay attention.** Make that **grand entrance** if that is what you want to do. **Demand** to have a voice but make **sure** to **use** it.

Travel to *exotic* places
sing at the top of your lungs
dance your ass off
hug hard, ***kiss passionately***
laugh so loud you shatter glass windows.
Whatever you do, ***hang the heck onto life***
and....

LIVE

OUT

LOUD!!!!

Finding the Power in My Pain

I *rise* again from beneath hurt so *big* it threatens to crush me to pieces as I shuffle from the *deepest depth* of me to keep my head above life's surface as I *battle those demons* trying to push me under.

I *push* with all that's in me to *escape* the painful aspects of an existence that is forcing me to stay afloat this shifting boat that is taking me on life's journey. I *propel* myself from under laden thoughts of despair - *challenging* the I in me to get up and *live*. I *drag* myself kicking and screaming from the fetters I place on my mind that keeps it *focused* only on past hurts and injustices real and imagined.

But then…..as I uncoil from my fetal position of vulerability, I *remind myself* that the pain I am feeling is *signaling* to me, the fact that I am *ready* to take on what is left to come, as now I have *mastered* the art of finding the power that lies in my pain……..

Not Looking Back...

as it *obscures* vision
and takes me too far away from the *goals* I am about to *achieve.*
There is nothing back there that I need to see
except to sear on my memory those *lessons I learnt -*
that will deter me from making the same mistakes I made before.

I will activate my rearview mirror
but *only* to *ensure* that there is nothing too close to me
that will *hinder* me from *fulfilling my dreams*;
and press on the reverse pedal only to pick up from where I left off in the *realization* of
a dream.

My *vision* is forward-looking;
looking in front of me to a **future that I am consciously creating -**
one that will *not* be left just to chance,
but one that is *guided* by the creator's plans for my life,
what I want for myself,
and one that will *always be fueled by possibilities of the endless kind*, because....
I am *not* looking back....

Duty Calls

ATTENTION……..
MARCH….
to the beat of *many* drums if you so choose, but moving to *your* specific tune to dance your way into doing *whatever* is necessary to move you in the direction *you* want to go
BY THE FRONT….
lead the pack that would strive to tear you to pieces rather than to have your back - away from your circle; your *space* of quietude and renewal by mere virtue of your *strength* of character.
HALTING ONLY….
to take a breath before moving on with the *business of living* and not merely *existing*.
RIGHT TURN….
away from mental boulders as you stop to smell the roses on your quest to break away from *uniformed* conformity.

MOVE TO THE LEFT….
of the *killers of your dreams* and….

PARADE….
your *gifts* and UTILIZE your talents; *never* being afraid to proclaim your *guard of honour* as a *worthy* member of the *universe* and of the *squad* of the *world*.
FALL IN….
but only when the conga line is playing the *music of life* that *you* prefer; that *you* want to hear.

CHANGE ARMS….
and do *about turns* when the usual and tested and *tried* paths no longer work for you and are a *hindrance* rather than a *propeller* to *bigger* and *better* things.
MARK TIME….
but only with the *expectation* of moving *forward* to your *best* life….
PACE….
if you must, but then do *double time* to make up for time lost and
MARCH ON….
in *whatever* steps that move you into the direction where your *dreams* await their *deserved* fulfillment….

*Love and romance are probably the biggest motivators
of human thoughts and actions there is.
Enjoy these pieces in anticipation of the publication
of my next book "Love-Speak"*

Cerebral Seduction

It starts in the mind—that mental stimulation that keeps brain cells pulsating to their own rhythm, and jiving to their own beats. An unexpected capture of that cerebral space, that goes into mental gymnastics from the caressing of its pinnacle.

Your brain does its victory jig as it welcomes those tantalizing words strung together to remove it from its self-induced coma, as it rolls off its lazy perch to respond to what has now become the master of its destiny!!!!.

Your mind is being bled of its restraint as you are hypnotically led into strands of sweetness by quivering thoughts and shivering imaginings, as you surrender to depths of sensation you didn't even know existed.

Love's MELODY

He plays me like an out-of-control fiddle, with the melodies haunting and piercing the deepest recesses of my wayward soul

He strums my "buttons" that are otherwise hidden from plain view, but that which are so exposed to him so that he can pluck at them so soulfully even with eyes closed and hands tied behind his back.

He beats that special sound on my heart that resonates within an alcove of tunes that have the same effect as whip cream on strawberries

He re-arranges the levels of my chords as he picks at the strings of my fully-surrendered heart, as I exhale in falsetto having lost the ability to be my own master.

We compose a duet that swells to a MIGHTY crescendo that alters the timing of our breathing, as we are taken to a space of expressionism wherein we can scarce contain the musical feelings within.

There are no flat areas in this musical interlude that is filled with a mixture of harmony, that modulates to keys higher than we thought we could reach.

There is no room for monotones, as the repertoire of his love-musicology is too vast to be subjected to repetitions.

He creates nocturnes that are meant only for me; that pushes me to octaves beyond my natural realm. I become an opera, an entire orchestra, where my pitch is extended to its contralto level and I am unable to operate my vocals normally.

I break into a recital of my deepest feelings as I try to match the rhythm of my own heartbeat. He serenades me as I slip into a symphony that is an expression of what is reverberating through my entire being.

The timbre of his harmonious strumming has now become the instrument of the power he holds over me, while I struggle against being completely saturated by his powerful melodies.

The tonality of his ability to "play me" is instrumental in visibly affecting the way I breathe, and I fight to stay on key as I lose control of my voice with vocal cords that have now become out of step with the erratic beating of my heart, but instead are absolutely in-tuned to him.

Strum me, play me, serenade the heck out of me, elevate me to a soprano as I RELISH in the feelings of the loss of all control when I surrender to the SWEETNESS of you!!.